Time for God

TIME FOR GOD

Guidelines for a full-time
or part-time retreat

by Edward Yarnold, SJ

'To him who conquers I will give some of the hidden manna,
and I will give him a white stone, with a new name written on
the stone which no one knows except him who receives it'
(Rev 2:17).

COLLINS

An earlier version of this book was published in Great Britain by the
Catholic Truth Society in 1984, under the title
EIGHT DAYS WITH THE LORD

This edition first published in Great Britain by
William Collins Sons & Co. Ltd, London in 1991,
and reprinted 1993 under the Collins imprint

Typesetting by Irish Typesetting and Publishing Co. Ltd, Galway
Printed and bound in Great Britain by
Bell & Bain Ltd, Glasgow

Scripture quotations (with very few exceptions)
are from the Revised Standard Version
Copyright © 1966 Division of Christian Education
of the National Council of the Churches of Christ in
the United States of America

The author gratefully acknowledges permission from Messrs Sheed and
Ward to quote from K. Rahner's *Spiritual Exercises* (pp. 41 and 115) and from
Alison Peers's translation of St Teresa's *Way of Perfection* (p. 91)

CONTENTS

INTRODUCTION

The desire to 'get away from it all' is one which we must all have felt. It prompts us to get away not only from our work-place but even from home when we can find time for a holiday. At a more profound level the same instinct underlay our Lord's invitation to his apostles to 'come away by yourselves to a lonely place and rest awhile' (Mk 6.31).

> The world is too much with us; late and soon,
> Getting and spending, we lay waste our powers.

Many Christians from all the churches feel the force of these words of Wordsworth, and take the opportunity of 'getting away'. This is the meaning of the word 'retreat' which is traditionally used to describe a period of spiritual holiday. It is an opportunity for a regathering of one's spiritual powers laid waste by getting and spending. People often refer to a retreat as a 'recharging of the batteries'. It is also a time for standing away from one's ordinary life in order to reappraise it with a critical eye, as a painter will stand back from his canvas in order to assess the general effect of the individual brush-strokes over which he has been poring so closely.

Above all a retreat is a *Time for God*. In our ordinary lives we too easily push God to the margins of our thoughts and desires and plans. In a retreat we allow him to come back to his rightful place in the centre; we spend a kind of 'second honeymoon' with him. This is another way of saying that in a retreat we are like the apostles looking forward to their holiday with Jesus; that we share with them their request: 'Lord, teach us to pray' (Lk 11:1).

This little book is a sort of guidebook for such a spiritual holiday; it provides hints and thoughts which it is hoped will help people to make a retreat. It is an exposition in my own terms of the greatest and most influential of all retreat guidebooks, the *Spiritual Exercises* written by Ignatius of Loyola, the sixteenth-century Basque saint who founded the Jesuit order. A Jesuit can scarcely help following his Founder's little book, not only out of loyalty, but because the *Exercises* have carved deep channels in his mind, along which his thought inevitably flows. But in any event the pattern of the *Exercises* is a natural one to follow, because the journey it outlines of conversion, followed by developing conformity to the Lord's life, death and resurrection, is simply the good news of the New Testament.

Precisely because the *Spiritual Exercises* are so biblical, I hope that these notes, which are based on the *Exercises*, will prove of use also to those who are not Roman Catholics, and who have never made an Ignatian retreat. I have seen at first hand how much help Anglicans and Free Church people can derive from making a retreat of this kind; and I have also seen how effectively such people can themselves guide others in an Ignatian retreat.

These notes are, precisely, notes. They provide outlines which you must fill in for yourselves. They will be of little use unless you use them with the Bible in front of you, and look up the passages quoted or referred to. But don't regard them as a lesson which has to be gone through from beginning to end. The notes are more like a menu to be selected from than a syllabus which has to be covered in full. Once the point has become clear, once you feel the wings of prayer beginning to spread, put the notes aside, put even the Bible aside, and simply pray. In the words of the negro spiritual, 'Every time I feel the Spirit moving in my heart, I will pray.'

PART-TIME OR FULL-TIME RETREAT?

This book is not designed for someone who is able to make the *Spiritual Exercises* in their ideal form by going away to a quiet place for a whole month where he or she can concentrate on the retreat without distractions. It is intended to meet two other needs: either for a shorter full-time retreat taking about eight days, or for a part-time retreat which is made in the middle of ordinary life by someone who can devote a regular period every day to prayer.

This second kind of retreat is one which Ignatius envisaged. He realized that many people would be unable to withdraw for several weeks from their ordinary occupations. He suggested therefore that, if they could find an hour and a half to spend on prayer each day and spread the *Exercises* over a longer period than a month, they could obtain much of the benefit of the more concentrated form of retreat. Since Ignatius explained this part-time method in the nineteenth of his preliminary notes, it is sometimes known as a 'Nineteenth Annotation Retreat'.

Many will find that even an hour and a half a day is not a realistic possibility. Much can be achieved if an hour a day is given to prayer. Even half an hour a day can bring results; but a shorter amount of time than that makes it hard to achieve the inner calm and concentration which the *Exercises* require.

Experience suggests that, while some people enter into a retreat more deeply if they are able to get away from their ordinary responsibilities and interests, others gain from the effort to pray in depth in the context of their ordinary lives. They are able to combine the advantage of 'standing back' from life with that of bringing their renewed familiarity with God into the midst of their daily occupations. A nineteenth annotation retreat therefore is not necessarily a second best, provided it is made with seriousness and generosity. Naturally, however, the practical difficulties are greater. In particular the family man or woman following this method will need some ingenuity in discovering a quiet time and place where they can pray without distraction, and great self-discipline in sticking faithfully to the daily period of prayer. Some people can manage to spend some time in a church every day. Those who can't do this may find it helpful to choose a quiet prayer-corner in their own home. It can be useful to have a centre of stillness and attention, such as an icon or a crucifix, or a lighted candle.

Those who are fortunate enough to be able to make a full-time retreat may be faced with the opposite difficulty: they may find themselves with an unaccustomed amount of time on their hands and not know how to fill it up. There will probably be a daily Eucharist, and perhaps the Church's morning and evening prayer. There will be three or four solid periods of prayer based on the notes. There will be the time needed for meals and chores. How do we spend the rest of the day? Here are two other activities that may prove valuable:

1.   It is helpful to walk outdoors in silence, letting the peace and joy of Christ sink into our hearts, and perhaps letting the thoughts that have struck us in reading the Bible or the notes, or, above all, in our prayer, stir gently in our minds without urgency or tension.

2.   It is valuable to have some spiritual book to read. However, during a retreat (outside a retreat things may be different) we do not read mainly for the sake of learning: a retreat should not be seen as an opportunity to catch up on our reading. The purpose is, above all, to avoid boredom, or, to put it less negatively, to pass some time in a relaxed way in the Lord's presence. It is better to have a book worth reading and which fits in with the general pattern of the retreat; and we may find God giving the words we are reading the power to stir our hearts or illuminate our understanding. But the main purpose, it seems to me, is to avoid 'the noonday devil', the sense of heaviness or spiritual repugnance, or the temptation to escape from the retreat by daydreaming or some other distraction.

THE SCHEME OF THIS BOOK

St Ignatius divided the full thirty-day Spiritual Exercises into four 'weeks' preceded by the 'Foundation'. He intended the 'weeks' to be interpreted flexibly, and varied according to the retreatant's needs, while envisaging that the whole process would be completed in about thirty days. I have followed a similar pattern in these notes, while preferring to speak of four 'parts' rather than 'weeks'. In order to help the retreatant to take the plunge I have placed before the Foundation some notes for an introductory period of prayer called 'Getting Started: Opening the Door'. At two points, after Part One and in the middle of Part Two, I have inserted 'Interludes' which may help the retreatant to think a little more deeply about what prayer is, and to cope with some of the difficulties which anyone who tries to pray seriously is likely to encounter.

Each part is divided into a number of sections, twenty-five in all. Those who wish to make a full-time eight-day retreat will thus find the introductory prayer on Opening the Door, plus three subjects for prayer a day. People who are making a nineteenth annotation retreat will naturally proceed more slowly. To help them to judge their pace three rules may prove helpful. The first rule is not to feel obliged to take the whole of a section each time; each section will contain enough matter for several days of prayer. The second rule is not to be afraid to go over the same matter more than once on successive days; it is especially worth while repeating a meditation if an idea has meant a lot to us, or if the contrary is true, and we feel any resistance to an idea that has been proposed. The third rule is not to move on to a new section until we can honestly say that we have received in some measure the grace for which we pray at the beginning of each prayer.

It is not always easy to judge whether we actually have received this grace sufficiently deeply for us to be ready to pass on to the next section. It will help, of course, if we have an experienced spiritual guide to advise us (more about this in the section on Getting Help). It may be that the effect which God is wanting to produce in us is not yet the precise grace for which we are praying, but rather the *desire* of it, and the determination to do what we can so as to be capable of receiving it in God's good time.

It can sometimes happen that before a nineteenth annotation retreat is over a person decides they have got as far as they are ready to go for the time being. If so, they should not force themselves on further than they can honestly go. They should round the retreat off at the point they have reached without any sense of failure, thanking God for what they have received, and leaving open the possibility of taking up the retreat again when they feel more ready for it. The main break-off point which St Ignatius envisages is the end of Part One.

USING THIS BOOK

But how should you pray? If you are already accustomed to spending longish periods in prayer, say half an hour or more, you will probably have found a method that suits you; so start with that. It may not be the method you end with, because the Holy Spirit may be wanting to lead you on to something different; but start from where you are at present. If you haven't yet discovered a method of prayer, the most important rule is to hold yourself quiet to hear the Holy Spirit.

It is always a mistake to be so afraid of emptiness or distraction that we spend the whole time reading either this book or another or even the Bible. The Holy Spirit does not usually speak to us miraculously: we don't *literally* hear him. He is much more likely to speak to us through the thoughts that rise in our minds quite naturally–though also supernaturally, as prayer is an exercise of grace. So to think over the ideas in these notes is to pray, if it is done in God's presence or, to put it another way, in pursuit of God's will. But if we do this it will be a good thing to spend part of the time not just thinking *about* God, but talking to him in our minds. Another way of praying is to hold ourselves in silence in God's presence, directing our attention by repeating rhythmically (though perhaps with long periods of silence in between) some text or ejaculatory prayer that sums up the particular grace we are seeking.

For in this kind of retreat each section, and therefore each period of prayer, is focused on one particular grace which I am seeking from God. It is for this reason that St Ignatius Loyola called his retreat notes *Spiritual Exercises*. Each meditation, like a physical exercise, is designed to produce a particular effect, though of course, unlike touching my toes, my efforts at prayer do not themselves produce the effect but are simply the occasion for the Holy Spirit to produce it by his grace.

The following might therefore be a good procedure:

1. Very briefly remind yourself of the presence of God who loves you, and ask the Holy Spirit for grace to pray.
2. Read the whole section through quickly.
3. Begin looking up the biblical references.
4. Jot down a few pregnant phrases that strike you. Let's call them *mantras*.
5. Put aside this book and the Bible, keeping only your *mantras* as you have written them down.
6. Pray for the particular grace suggested in the notes.
7. Take the first of your *mantras* and think about it, or talk to God about it, or simply be still, repeating it occasionally in your mind.
8. If one *mantra* is enough, spend the entire time on it. If you feel you have got all you need out of your first *mantra*, then go on to the second.
9. It is useful to conclude with one, two or three short vocal prayers, perhaps the *Memorare*, the *Anima Christi*, and the Lord's Prayer (see Appendix).
10. End crisply. Don't drift out of prayer.
11. Say the briefest 'Thank you' to God for the gift of prayer.
12. It is a good idea to find time to consider whether you could improve your method of prayer.

The foregoing procedure has been based on the presupposition that the basis of prayer will be words: the words of scripture or the words which express our own reaction to it. (I say 'basis', but it might be more accurate to say 'starting-point', for we must allow God to lead us in prayer where he chooses, and not stifle the Spirit by refusing to budge from a familiar system of prayer.) This word-focused type of prayer is for most people the most suitable for the opening stages of the retreat. There is however another, more imaginative, type, which consists in making ourselves witnesses of a scene in the gospels, and even participants in it. This form of prayer is most appropriate to the later stages of the retreat. The retreatant is introduced to it in Section 10.

KEEPING A RECORD

If any ideas have struck us during prayer, it is useful to note them down soon afterwards. It sometimes happens that prayer itself is a time of desire rather than of discovery, and that our understanding of God seems to develop more readily outside the period of formal prayer. The action of writing can both clarify our thoughts and stimulate their flow. It can help us to make whatever decisions we have to make, and can also be a means by which the Holy Spirit instructs us. Many people keep these jottings in the form of a simple diary, to which they can refer later in order to revive their memory of a privileged time of light. Of course we must not allow ourselves to be distracted from essentials by the desire to produce a literary composition; the sole aim is to provide for ourselves an unpretentious and clear record of the truth as God seems to be showing it to us.

But the most important things to note are not so much ideas as our reactions to them. Some thoughts may have aroused in us a sense of rightness, of peace, of joy, or of spiritual energy. By contrast we may find that other thoughts leave us with a sense of uneasiness or depression or repulsion or fear. Either reaction is an indication that the thought in question is not just a matter of abstract interest to us but affects our very selves. A sense of peace, for example, is probably a sign that a thought is in harmony with a deep-seated attitude or tendency or instinct; but it is not always easy to tell whether this instinct is one which urges us to serve God and follow Christ or whether it is a selfish instinct to put our own interests first. Again the sense of disturbance is probably due to a resistance in our personalities to the thought in question; but does the resistance to the thought arise from our desire to serve God or from our ingrained selfishness? It may be vitally important for us to be able to answer these questions. It can be fatal to take a sense of peace as an infallible guide to God's will. St Ignatius gave much thought to this question of 'discernment of spirits' (the term is first found in 1 Cor 12:10; cf. Heb 5:14; 1 Jn 4:1); on p. 53 I have given extracts from his treatment of the subject. Sometimes we can quickly recognize whether these reactions arise from our generous or our selfish ideals; sometimes it can take much prayer and thought and considerable time. To clarify and record our reactions unpretentiously in writing helps us both to discern the spirits for ourselves, and to explain our reactions to a spiritual guide if we decide to seek advice.

DECISION-MAKING

Often a retreat will be a time of decision. If we have any spiritual anxieties or doubts, a retreat is a time of light and grace when we can make at least the first step towards a solution. Sometimes we may be faced with a decision which will determine the shape of the rest of our lives. Traditionally, this is called an '*election*'. For example, is God calling me to serve him as a member of a religious order or as a layperson? Should I close one chapter in my life and start a new one by taking some irreversible action–

for example, giving up a job, or disposing of some property? Decision-making of this kind fits in best in Part Two, and is discussed at that point in the notes.

There is another kind of decision which is required of us nearly every time we make a retreat. There are usually faults which need to be put right in our lives, or steps which we need to take if we are to serve God more faithfully. In that case, we need to make a *resolution*–say, to spend less money on beer or tobacco, to get up promptly in the morning, or to stop discussing other people's faults. The more concrete the resolution is, the better. It is more effective to resolve not to pull my friends to pieces when I travel to work with so-and-so on the bus, than it is simply to resolve to avoid gossip in general. You have to keep a check on your resolution. It is a good plan to remind yourself of it every morning, if anything is to get done (again, this should be done at a precise time–for example, while you are cleaning your teeth), and to assess your performance every night (see pp. 51–53).

A third kind of decision always needs to be made. This is a reaffirmation of our dedication to Christ, such as we make in renewing our baptismal promises at Easter. Any practical decision we make of the first or second kind will simply be the concrete expression of this basic commitment. Even if we do not see the need to make any immediate practical decision, making a retreat properly will always involve the renewal of this fundamental dedication.

Some people find it helpful to clarify their dedication to Christ by choosing some particular text which seems to sum up the way God has been leading them during the retreat. This choice of a particular emphasis in the following of Christ can be seen as a fourth kind of decision. For example, we may have come to see each detail of our lives as an invitation to do our heavenly Father's will; in that case we might choose as our motto the text: 'My food is to do the will of him who sent me' (Jn 4:34). We might feel called to serve Christ through serving our neighbour; such an ideal could be summed up in our Lord's words: 'As you did it to one of the least of these my brethren, you did it to me' (Mt 25:40). We might wish to make our lives an attempt to accept Jesus' invitation to take up our cross and follow him (Mk 8:34). Other people might find that their decision is more powerfully expressed by a visual symbol, such as a white stone (Rev 2:17) or a pearl (Mt 13:46), or by a particular person in the Gospel, such as Mary who sat at Jesus' feet and chose the 'good portion' (Lk 10:39–42).

GETTING HELP

I might have called this book simply *A Do-It-Yourself Retreat*, but someone else thought of that first. Anyhow, that title would have had its dangers, because if one thing is certain about making a retreat it is that you can't be sure of doing it yourself. Most people making a serious retreat find they need to talk over some problems with someone they can trust. It is clearly an advantage if you can find a 'spiritual guide' or 'soul-friend' who has some experience in the giving of retreats; but even if such an experienced person is not available, it is often better to speak to any Christian whose judgment you respect than to keep uncertainties to yourself. Not that you can pass your responsibility for your own decisions to anybody else; but simply to express your problem to someone else, even if you think you know the answer already, can help you to see the problem more clearly. Discussion like this can be an occasion for facing God honestly and humbly, and for freeing ourselves from inertia.

In addition, people who belong to a church in which confession is practised will probably find this sacrament a great help, especially when their prayer is turned towards sin and forgiveness in Part One. However the roles of the retreat guide and the confessor are distinct, though they may overlap. The retreat guide's task is to help the retreatant to pray and to recognize God's will; the confessor brings to the sinful retreatant

God's forgiveness and his healing. But both processes, of guidance and reconciliation, require the retreatant to recognize and humbly to acknowledge the unvarnished truth about himself or herself.

THE SPIRITUAL EXERCISES

This book can be used without any reference to the *Spiritual Exercises*, but for those who wish to supplement the notes by reading what Ignatius himself wrote I have reproduced, where appropriate, extracts from the Ignatian text. Readers should be warned, however, that in places they may have to dig away layers of puzzling sixteenth-century theology and uncongenial baroque imagery in order to bring to light the treasure hidden underneath. I have made the translation myself, aiming at simplicity and clarity rather than literal accuracy. Those who would like a more exact rendering might turn to any one of a number of modern accurate translations, such as that by William Yeomans.

In addition at the end of each section I have printed a poem which seems appropriate for that particular stage along the spiritual journey. A poem can help us to feel with our hearts what otherwise we would only grasp with our reason. St Ignatius again and again spoke of the need for the retreatant to 'taste' or 'savour' the truth. Poetry can help us to acquire this spiritual sensitivity.

GETTING STARTED

1. OPENING THE DOOR

1. 'And someone said to him, "Lord, will those who are saved be few?" And he said to them, "Strive to enter by the narrow door; for many, I tell you, will seek to enter and will not be able. When once the householder has risen up and shut the door, you will begin to stand outside and to knock at the door, saying 'Lord, open to us.' He will answer you, 'I do not know where you come from'"' (Lk 13:23–5). Englishmen, we like to think, don't push, but form an orderly queue so that everyone passes through the narrow door in turn. Picture instead an Italian bus with everyone pushing to get in, because there are only a few places; then the bus door shuts, and it is no use battering at the glass. Fight your way in at the narrow door–not, I think, because the places in heaven are limited, but because we will only get there if we have as much urgency *as if* there were only room for a few. It is with this spirit of urgency that we need to come to a retreat.

2. St Paul strikes the same note of urgency in his famous words, 'Work out your own salvation with fear and trembling' (Phil 2:12). When making a retreat we need to focus all our energies on the task in hand, as a burning-glass focuses the rays of the sun to a point of incandescent power. We have two things to do in retreat: to pray and to listen. To pray: to seek God in prayer with all our hearts. To listen: for we may not rest content with our own idea of God, but need constantly to listen to him as he speaks in scripture, in what we read and hear, and in our hearts, showing himself to us as he is, not as perhaps, in our cowardice, we would like him to be. We need to listen also because he may be asking something of us. Work out your salvation for yourself with fear and trembling; fight your way in; effort, concentration.

3. There is another passage in the New Testament about

knocking, only now it is not ourselves but Christ who knocks. 'Behold I stand at the door and knock; if anyone hears my voice and opens the door, I will come in to him and eat with him, and he with me' (Rev 3:20). He is locked out from our hearts unless we choose to open them. We may be afraid of what he has to tell us if we open the door to that knock; we may be tempted to turn up the radio so that we won't hear the door-bell when he rings. But we have no need to be afraid. He always comes like a telegraph-boy with a greetings telegram; the news he brings is always good, the Gospel, the good spell, the good news.

4.   The passage from Philippians doesn't stop at the fear and trembling. It goes on: '. . . For God is at work in you, both to will and to work for his good pleasure' (Phil 2:13). St Paul is not telling us that if anxiously and painfully we first do our part, then God will reward our efforts with his saving grace. On the contrary, our efforts and even our desires from the very first are the product of God's power energizing us. So the urgent efforts we make during a retreat are not the frantic clawings of a non-swimmer afraid of drowning, but the steady, confident, powerful stroke of one who knows that the water is a friend supporting him, not an enemy seeking to overwhelm him; like a yacht gliding swiftly and silently before a fresh breeze, with none of the straining of the canvas and the tensions in the shrouds of a boat tacking against the wind, fighting for every yard. Prayer, like good singing, requires effort but not strain; strain is a sign that we are trying to force God's grace according to our own preconceptions, instead of trying to strike out with God's tide.

5.   Why are we making this effort? What is the aim of a retreat? Retreat-making is not a self-centred activity. Our aim is not to cultivate our own souls for our own sake. We are not striving for a *thing* called holiness or perfection. We are looking for a *person*, God, and trying to know him better and love him more. Besides, the more we grow in the love of God, the more we are capable of

helping other people. We can make our own Jesus' words: 'For their sake I consecrate myself, that they also may be consecrated in truth' (Jn 17:19).

6.   The quality that is needed most of all in one entering into a retreat is *desire*. If we *really* want to grow in love of God we will. 'There are very few people who realize what God would make of them if they abandoned themselves entirely into his hands, and let themselves be formed by his grace' (St Ignatius of Loyola). 'As much as we hope for from God we shall receive.' 'God says you can have anything on the shelf provided you are prepared to pay.' Even this desire is a grace for which we must pray; we cannot achieve it for ourselves. I may be afraid of growing in the love of God. I may not even be able to say I want to grow in his love. But at least I can pray that I may want to do so.

7.   Iris Murdoch says in one of her novels: 'In order to become good it may be necessary to imagine oneself good' (*The Nice and the Good*, Penguin ed., p.77). It might be useful if we imagined what it would be like if we said Yes to God–not what a hypothetical saint in my situation would be like, but what *I* would be like, with all my fears and love of my own comfortable groove, as well as with my abilities and potentialities. Then, having envisaged this as an abstract possibility, I might admit it into my reckoning as a *real* possibility for myself. And then, however much it frightens me, I might pray that this possibility might come true–provided it really is God's will, for his will does not always coincide with our understanding of it, however hard we try to free ourselves from our preconceptions.

From the Spiritual Exercises of St Ignatius:

Annotation 5: It will be very profitable for a person who is being given the Exercises if he sets out with a great and generous spirit towards his Creator and Lord, and offers him his whole will and his liberty, allowing God to dispose freely of himself and of all he possesses, according to his most holy will (n.5).

From *The Wreck of the Deutschland*

With an anvil-ding
and with fire in him forge thy will
Or rather, rather then, stealing as Spring
Through him, melt him but master him still:
Whether at once, as once at a crash Paul,
Or as Austin, a lingering-out swéet skíll,
make mercy in all of us, out of us all
Mastery, but be adored, but be adored King.

GERARD MANLEY HOPKINS

THE FOUNDATION: GOD

2. GOD OUR CREATOR

1. In this first meditation the grace we seek is a deeper understanding of the otherness of God, the infinite gap between ourselves and him. We are not for the moment considering the fact of sin, which establishes a gap of personal apartness between ourselves and God–a gap erected solely by our disobedience and rejection of his love (we shall consider this later)–but rather the fact that God is himself, the 'Almighty Father, Creator of heaven and earth,' as we say in the Creed, and I am myself, God's creation.

2. I have no rights before God; I am completely in his power, as a man with lifted foot has it totally in his power to crush an ant. If God took back the breath of life, then everything living would die (cf. Job 34:14). And not only in his physical power; it is not only a question of might, but also of right. As a character in a novel has no appeal against its author who may determine its development, condemn it to praise or blame, happiness or misery, so God not only *can* but has the *right* to do what he chooses with me. The only restraints on the author are the need to write a book which will sell, and his artistic sense. With God the first kind of restraint is absent as he gains nothing from creating me. He knows no constraint apart from his own nature. He is all-good as well as all-powerful, and *cannot* abuse his power over me.

3. So his *power* over me is unlimited: 'It is he who sits above the circle of the earth, and its inhabitants are like grasshoppers' (Is 40:22). The *rightness* of his action is beyond one's questioning: the Lord answered Job out of the whirlwind, 'Shall a faultfinder contend with the Almighty?' What he does is right because he does it (Job 40:1). He has no moral standards to conform to. But

above all I am content to be in God's hands, because he is good. 'The *faithfulness* of the Lord endures forever' (Ps 117:2).

4.   God is the *Other*, then, in the sense that he is beyond all the limits of power as we know them, and beyond all moral questioning–his right and his goodness are rock-like facts. He is also the Other in the sense that he is a hidden God. The Old Testament writers expressed this fact by such stories as that of Moses being hidden in the cleft of the rock where his eyes were covered by God lest he should see God's face. 'No one has ever seen God' (Jn 1:18). God 'dwells in unapproachable light', and 'no man has ever seen or can see' him (1 Tim 6:16). Our knowledge and our language are based on experience: God is too great for our experience, and our words can make only the most inadequate attempts at describing him. Our efforts to do justice to God in words are like attempts to play a Beethoven symphony on a dustbin lid. A child is not capable of the emotional experience of an adult: a little girl playing with a doll may be copying her mother, but she has only a remote inkling of her mother's experience. Multiply by infinity this gap of incomprehension between a child and an adult, and you will arrive at some idea of the gap between God and our knowledge, some idea of God's otherness.

5.   It follows from all this that the proper attitude of a human being before God is flat on his face in adoration. Our prayer is above all *worship*. Even if we seem to receive no spiritual benefit from prayer, we are by our efforts adoring God. To pray is not only to converse and to experience: it is to *do* something, namely to fulfil our duty of worshipping God.

6.   Another way of putting it is to say we give God glory. 'Glory to God in the highest,' the angels sang on Christmas night (Lk 2:14). St Ignatius's motto was, 'for the greater glory of God'. We glorify God not in a servile spirit, but in a spirit of love. We are glad he is what he is; 'We give you thanks for your great glory.'

7.   Yet God for all his apartness from us did not remain aloof from us. For all his hiddenness he did not remain in darkness. 'God so loved the world that he gave his only Son' (Jn 3:16). He wanted to reveal himself to us so much that he became one of us, so as to 'make himself known' (cf. Jn 1:18). But of this later.

God moves in a mysterious way

God moves in a mysterious way
  His wonders to perform;
He plants His footsteps in the sea,
  And rides upon the storm.

Deep in unfathomable mines
  Of never failing skill
His treasures up His bright designs,
  And works His sovereign will.

Ye fearful saints, fresh courage take:
  The clouds ye so much dread
Are big with mercy, and shall break
  In blessings on your head.

Judge not the Lord by feeble sense,
  But trust Him for His grace;
Behind a frowning providence
  He hides a smiling face.

His purposes will ripen fast,
  Unfolding ev'ry hour;
The bud may have a bitter taste,
  But sweet will be the flow'r.

Blind unbelief is sure to err,
 And scan His work in vain;
God is His own interpreter,
 And He will make it plain.

WILLIAM COWPER

3. GOD OUR FATHER

1. In this meditation we seek again the grace of a grateful and deeper understanding of our relationship with God. In the first meditation we considered the otherness of God: now we consider how God bridged the gap—when he took our human nature he imparted to us a share of his divinity, as the priest says quietly at Mass when putting the drops of water into the wine which is to become the means of Christ's presence. What we seek is the grace to relax trustfully and contentedly in the hands of God. Let us humble ourselves beneath the hand of God. 'His will is our peace.' 'Lord, to whom whall we go? You have the words of eternal life' (Jn 6:68).

2. In the Old Testament there were already intimations of this new relationship between God and the human beings he had created. This new relationship was offered to the Israelites, and, as some of the prophets saw, the Israelites were to be the means of bringing the whole human race a share in it. It was essentially the enjoyment of a privilege, a gift: the Israelites were chosen to receive it, they were God's special possession. The relationship was embodied in the covenant between God and his people, a treaty to which God would never cease to be 'faithful'. God was his people's King, or Shepherd, or Husband, the people were his flock, his bride, his vine. His love was even greater and more enduring than the love of a mother for her children (Is 49:15).

3. Because of the Incarnation the New Testament has a far deeper insight into God's love for his people: God is our Father. The Sermon on the Mount develops this theme in many ways. God cares for each one of us with a loving providence; more than

the flowers which he makes to grow, more than the birds, none of which can die without his knowledge. 'How much more you, you of little faith' (Mt 6:30).

4. God's fatherhood, however, means much more than this; it implies the doctrine of the Trinity. God is our heavenly Father, because he is Jesus' Father–'I am ascending to my Father and your Father' (Jn 20:17). St Paul speaks often of the fact that we are *adopted* sons and daughters of God. St John expresses a similar idea, while emphasizing that this adoption is not a legal arrangement (as we understand adoption). Good fosterparents can forge a relationship similar to that of natural parenthood with their adopted children, but they can never become the parents. With God and ourselves it is different: 'See what love the Father has given us, that we should be called children of God; *and so we are*' (1 Jn 3:1).

5. It is God the Holy Spirit who makes us a 'new creation' (2 Cor 5:17), so that we may become truly sons and daughters of God. 'For all who are led by the Spirit of God are sons of God. For you did not receive the spirit of slavery to fall back into fear, but you have received the spirit of sonship. When we cry "Abba! Father!", it is the Spirit himself bearing witness with our spirit that we are children of God' (Rom 8:14–16).

6. We are used to calling God our Father, but it would be an extremely presumptuous thing to do if we did not have our Lord's word for it. This is why, from very early in the Church's history, Christians, before saying the Lord's Prayer at the Eucharist, have reminded themselves of the liberty they were taking. At present the introductory words go like this: 'Let us pray with confidence to the Father in the words our Saviour gave us.' More literally, the Latin original says: 'Instructed as we are by our Saviour's command and taught by divine direction we *make bold* to say: Our Father.'

From *The Wreck of the Deutschland*

Thou mastering me
God! giver of breath and bread;
World's strand, sway of the sea;
Lord of living and dead;
Thou hast bound bones and veins in me, fastened me flesh,
And after it almost unmade, what with dread,
Thy doing: and dost thou touch me afresh?
Over again I feel thy finger and find thee.

I am soft sift
In an hourglass—at the wall
Fast, but mined with a motion, a drift,
And it crowds and it combs to the fall;
I steady as a water in a well, to a poise, to a pane,
But roped with, always, all the way down from the tall
Fells or flanks of the voel, a vein
Of the gospel proffer, a pressure, a principle, Christ's gift.

I kiss my hand
To the stars, lovely-asunder
Starlight, wafting him out of it; and
Glow, glory in thunder;
Kiss my hand to the dappled-with-damson west:
Since, tho' he is under the world's splendour and wonder,
His mystery must be instressed, stressed;
For I greet him the days I meet him, and bless when I
understand.

GERARD MANLEY HOPKINS

B

4. OUR RESPONSE

1.   In this meditation the grace we seek is the right response to the love God has shown in creating us; first, as before, a conviction that it is right that I should try to fulfil the will of so loving and wise a Creator; secondly, the joyful resolve to put the conviction into practice.

2.   Why did God make me? The question can be taken in two ways:
(a) What is God's motive in creating me, sustaining me in being, and redeeming me?
(b) What are God's intentions for me?
     Let us answer these two questions separately.

3.   (a) God does not need to create. The inner life of the three Persons in one God is not monotonous or unfulfilling; God does not need to create for the sake of a hobby or in order to have servants to perform his will. God created us because he is essentially a giving God. 'God is Love' (1 Jn 4:16). But he is a God who does not *need* to give. His only motive is Love, without any of the psychological need to love and be loved that always enters into our loving.

4.   (b) God's intention for me is summed up in the two great commandments: 'You shall love the Lord your God with all your heart, and with all your soul, and with all your mind. This is the great and first commandment. And a second is like it, You shall love your neighbour as yourself' (Mt 22:37–9). The commandments coincide (the second is *like* the first). Love of God is not abstract and disembodied: it is by loving our neighbour that our love of God is expressed, as I cannot play a tune without playing an instrument.

5.   The question of God's intention can be approached from another angle. It is never enough to say that God made us to love one another: to say that God made A to love B, and B to love A does not answer the question why God *wants* this love. Although, as we have just seen, God's love of us is an ultimate fact, God's will that we should love one another is not. It must depend on the ulterior fact that it is good for us to love and be loved. God made us to be united with him and one another in heaven; we have to grow as loving persons in this life, for only such persons can 'enter into the joy of the Lord' (cf. Mt 25:21). To change the metaphor, this life is a pilgrimage; it is love which brings us to our destination.

6.   Within this scheme of things the other works of God's creation have their place. Human beings have a value for their own sake; but other created things exist for the sake of man. They are the raw material of man's growth. In Teilhard de Chardin's words, they have a spiritual power. We should use them, not like an aesthete seeking new experiences, but as the means by which we can serve our fellow men. 'Everything works for good with those who love God' (Rom 8:28).

7.   This philosophy of creation requires us to see all God's creatures in this context *and to make our choices accordingly*. We should not be puffed about by every passing whim. Every choice should be made for God and for our fellow men. We shall, of course, often choose to do what we want to do; but in so far as we live as God's creation, we shall do so only if, and only because, this is what love of God and love of our neighbour require. This would, of course, involve great sanctity; but with the help of grace our motives can become progressively purer and less selfish provided our vision of the spiritual significance of things develops.

8.   We will always have natural inclinations; we need them, we

would not be human without them. But we must not follow them heedlessly. Often, of course, decisions must be instantaneous, and will be made in the light of our habitual values. But when we are faced with the need for a considered decision, we should be poised before the alternatives, so that the balance of our choice is tipped not by inclination but by the consideration of the demands of love. However, though we should be poised when deciding what God's will is, we should be far from poised in our urge towards it. We should be like homing pigeons circling in the sky, until discovering in what direction home lies; but once it is discovered hesitation is past, and they speed to their destination. It should be with us as with G. M. Hopkins:

> My heart, but you were dovewinged, I can tell,
> Carrier-witted, I am bold to boast.
>
> ('The Wreck of the Deutschland')

9.   I might pray for light to know myself better, to discover what motives disturb my poise, making me tend to seek my own preferences rather than God's will.

From the Spiritual Exercises of St Ignatius:

FIRST PRINCIPLE AND FOUNDATION

We human beings were created to praise reverence and serve our Lord and God, and in this way to save our souls. Everything else on the face of the earth was created for our sake to help us to attain the end for which we were created. It follows that we ought to use these other created things in so far as they help us reach this goal and refrain from using them in so far as they impede us. Consequently we ought to hold ourselves equally poised before each created thing (in so far as this is open to our free choice and not forbidden), so that, in so far as in us lies, we do not seek health more than illness, or prefer wealth to poverty, or honours to contempt, or a long life to a short one, etc. We should desire and choose only those things which help us to attain our end (n.23).

From *The Wreck of the Deutschland*

> I did say yes
> O at lightning and lashed rod;
> Thou heardst me truer than tongue confess
> Thy terror, O Christ, O God;
> Thou knowest the walls, altar and hour and night:
> The swoon of a heart that the sweep and the hurl of thee trod
> Hard down with a horror of height:
> And the midriff astrain with leaning of, laced with fire of stress.
>
> The frown of his face
> Before me, the hurtle of hell
> Behind, where, where was a, where was a place?
> I whirled out wings that spell
> And fled with a fling of the heart to the heart of the Host.
> My heart, but you were dovewinged, I can tell,
> Carrier-witted, I am bold to boast,
> To flash from the flame to the flame then, tower from the grace
> to the grace.

GERARD MANLEY HOPKINS

PART ONE: SIN AND FORGIVENESS

5. THE FOLLY OF SIN

1. The grace I pray for is that I may understand sin more clearly, so as to come to a deeper sorrow for my own sins, a sorrow leading to love for the redeemer who died to save me.

2. It appears that many people today, even good, believing Christians, have lost the sense of sin. This may be due to bad psychology, which leads them to believe that all sense of guilt is harmful; it may be due to bad theology, as if the death and resurrection of Christ had eliminated the fact of sin, or as if the virtue of hope drove out the virtue of contrition.

3. However the emphasis of the New Testament and the liturgy is quite different. Jesus is so called because he is to save his people from their sins (Mt 1:21). If we say there is no sin in us we make him a liar (1 Jn 1:10; read the whole chapter). The Eucharist begins with a service of penance: 'To prepare ourselves to celebrate the sacred mysteries, let us call to mind our sins.' Christ is the Lamb of God, who takes away the sin of the world (Jn 1:29). In other words, if we want to know the essential fact about Jesus, it is that he is the Saviour, the Mediator: 'God was in Christ reconciling the world to himself' (2 Cor 5:19). 'The saying is sure and worthy of full acceptance, that Christ Jesus came into the world to save sinners' (1 Tim 1:15).

4. Sin then is not an amiable weakness, like that of a child. Sin 'is not a trick of God's love that he uses to show us our poverty and creaturehood so that he can show us how merciful he is' (Karl Rahner, *Spiritual Exercises*, p.36). 'Are we to continue in sin that grace may abound?' asks St Paul, and gives the answer, 'By no means' (Rom 6:1–2). Sin is not the prelude to grace: it repels grace.

5.   Sin is folly. Folly because it is the defiance of the Almighty: 'It is a fearful thing to fall into the hands of the living God' (Heb 10:31). It is a rejection of the plan of the all-wise and all-loving God. Like Esau we sell our birthright for a meal. Sin is failure in life; failure to become what God wants us to become; failure to serve others as God wants us to. The one thing that even God cannot obtain for himself is my love, and by sin I refuse this.

6.   Does God make good my failures? In my own spiritual development, perhaps; certainly he forgives them if I let him. But the harm my sin has done to others sometimes seems to remain even after I repent; sinful or careless parents, for example, can distort their child's character, and leave it marked in its deepest self for life. Perhaps purgatory is the process by which the harm I have done to others is healed in them as well as in me.

From the Spiritual Exercises of St Ignatius:

THE FIRST MEDITATION ON SIN

The preparatory prayer consists of asking our Lord God for the grace that all our intention, energy and actions may tend solely to his service and praise (n.46).

The first prelude consists of placing oneself in a setting. In every contemplation or meditation on a visible subject, such as Christ our Lord in his humanity, we should set before our imagination a concrete place containing the subject of our prayer, such as a temple or a mountain, where we can find Jesus Christ or the Virgin Mary or whatever subject we wish to contemplate. But if we are reflecting on an abstract subject, such as in the present consideration of sin, the composition of place will consist of visualizing our soul confined in this corruptible body, and imagining humanity exiled in both body and soul among brute beasts in this valley of misery (n.47).

The second prelude will consist of asking our Lord God for what I desire, according to the subject matter of the meditation. For example, if I am going to pray about the resurrection, I should ask for a joy which is a share in the joy of Christ; if on the passion, for anguish, tears and suffering, so as to share the suffering of Christ. Accordingly in the present meditation I should ask for shame and confusion when I consider how many people have been damned for one mortal sin, and how often I have deserved eternal damnation for the many sins I have committed (n.48).

Colloquy. I will imagine Jesus Christ present before me, nailed to the cross, and ask why the Creator deigned to become human and to pass from eternal life to temporal death for my sins. I will consider myself, asking what I have done for Christ, what I am doing for Christ, and what I ought to do for Christ. Thus, fixing my gaze on him nailed to the cross, I shall say what comes into my mind (n.53).

In general the colloquy is like the conversation of a friend with a friend or a servant with his master, sometimes asking for some favour, sometimes acknowledging some fault, sometimes speaking of his affairs and asking for advice. To conclude, one should say the Our Father (n.54).

St Peter

St Peter once: 'Lord, dost Thou wash my feet?'—
   Much more I say: Lord, dost Thou stand and knock
   At my closed heart more rugged than a rock,
Bolted and barred, for Thy soft touch unmeet,
Nor garnished nor in any wise made sweet?
   Owls roost within and dancing satyrs mock.
   Lord, I have heard the crowing of the cock
And have not wept: ah, Lord, thou knowest it.

Yet still I hear Thee knocking, still I hear:
　'Open to Me, look on Me eye to eye,
That I may wring thy heart and make it whole;
And teach thee love because I hold thee dear
　And sup with thee in gladness soul with soul,
And sup with thee in glory by and by.'

CHRISTINA ROSSETTI

6. THE MALICE OF SIN

1.   The grace for which we pray is again the understanding of sin, leading to contrition and to love of our Saviour. The understanding of sin requires faith. Even if we may be able to reach a theoretical understanding of it by unaided human reason, that is not enough: for this to become a living knowledge, capable of influencing our lives, we need revelation and grace. Therefore we need to *pray* for this understanding, for it is God's gift, and a precious one, not something we can achieve for ourselves.

2.   In order to convince someone of the danger of driving without a seatbelt, you might take him to an accident ward and show him casualties with their faces in stitches because they had gone through the windscreen. Most of us are naturally inert and optimistic, and take a lot of persuading about the ill-effects of something we can't be bothered giving up; so let us consider the effects of sin.

3.   First, the effect it can have on a personality. Sin is not basically the breaking of a rule, whether God-made or man-made; it is the selfish refusal to love. Each individual choice of ours helps to carve lines on our personalities. Each sin makes us a less loving person. We all know how particular sins can wreck a character: lying, for example, or laziness, or self-indulgence. More subtle is the way in which our repeated selfish choices can make us into a selfish person, although there may be no obvious viciousness or bad habits in our lives. 'Men loved darkness rather than light, because their deeds were evil. For everyone who does evil hates the light' (Jn 3:19–20).

4.   The doctrine of hell is the ultimate expression of belief in the

effect of sins. The gospels attribute many sayings about hell to our Lord. We should think of hell not so much as a punishment for sin as the effect of sin. We damn ourselves. We kill the life of grace in our souls, drive out the Holy Spirit, cut ourselves off from the Body of Christ. Sartre said that hell is other people, but it is, rather, ourselves. 'Why, this is hell, nor am I out of it,' said Marlowe's Mephistopheles. If all human moral goodness is the result of grace (even in those who would not profess to be Christians), absence of grace means absence of moral goodness. 'Depart from me, you cursed, into the eternal fire' (Mt 25:41). 'Their worm does not die, and the fire is not quenched' (Mk 9:48; cf. 9:42–50).

5.   It does not follow that one cannot make this meditation unless one is aware of mortal sins in one's own life. Mortal sin cannot be incurred lightly, since it is cutting oneself off from all that is good. Mortal sin may be rare. We can never tell what a person's subjective dispositions are when he commits what appears to be a grave sin. Venial sin will be the subject of our next meditation. For the time being it is enough to see every sin, even venial, as a rejection of God, even though the rejection may be less than total. Just as there is an affinity between a small act of spite and murder, as in both cases we wish the other harm, so there is between a venial sin and the totally disastrous rejection of God which sets us in hell.

6.   Some time in these days it may be helpful to examine our consciences, asking for the grace to know ourselves better, and to discover sins we were unaware of. We should look especially for sins of omission (not 'what I have done', but 'what I have failed to do'), for they may fit less obviously into the ordinary categories, and so are less easily noticed. In my dealings with X, Y and Z, in my duties as this and that, am I meeting the requirements of love?

7.   Confession can also be a help at this stage, for those who

belong to a church which practises this rite. It is the sacrament of forgiveness. It reminds us of the social aspect of sin. My sin affects others as well as myself. Since sin is a refusal to love, and our sinfulness weakens the whole Church, we seek Christ's forgiveness through reconciliation with the Church we have hurt by our selfishness. The priest in pronouncing absolution is reconciling us with the whole Church.

8.   The overwhelming evidence of the effect of sin is Calvary. My sins were part of the cause of Jesus' suffering. To sin is not to 'crucify again the Son of God' (cf. Heb 6:6), this is impossible; nor does each sin *add* to what Christ suffered. But each sin is an act of solidarity with the evil which caused Christ to suffer; there is a callousness and cynicism in every sin.

9.   We should perhaps end, though, with the consideration of the immense love of Christ for us, who died on the cross to save us. 'While we were yet helpless, at the right time Christ died for the ungodly. Why, one will hardly die for a righteous man— though perhaps for a good man one will dare even to die' (Rom 5.6–7). We might imagine ourselves like the woman taken in adultery, standing before Jesus, knowing our guilt and hearing his words: 'Neither do I condemn you; go, and do not sin again' (Jn 8:11).

From the Spiritual Exercises of St Ignatius:

The fifth point is to cry out in wonder and keen emotion, calling to mind all created things and marvelling that they have supported me for so long and preserved my life–how the angels, who are the sword of the divine justice, have dared to support me, protected me, and even helped me with their prayers; how the saints have interceded and prayed for me; how the sky, the sun, the moon and the stars, the elements, the fruits of the earth, the birds, the fishes and animals have served me; finally how the earth has not opened to swallow me up, creating new hells for my eternal punishment (n.60).

The meditation will end with a colloquy in which I consider God's mercy, thank him for allowing me to live till today, and resolve to amend my ways for the future (n.61).

From *Doctor Faustus*

FAUSTUS

How comes it, then, that thou art out of hell?

MEPHISTOPHELES:

Why, this is hell, nor am I out of it.
Think'st thou that I, who saw the face of God,
And tasted the eternal joys of heaven,
Am not tormented with ten thousand hells,
In being depriv'd of everlasting bliss?
Oh, Faustus, leave these frivolous demands,
Which strike a terror to my fainting soul.

CHRISTOPHER MARLOWE

7. VENIAL SIN AND COURAGE

1. The sin we experience most is venial sin. The grace we seek in this meditation is twofold. First we ask for the grace to recognize our own venial sins, and to repent and amend. Secondly we ask for courage in the face of them; for a large number of good people are depressed and inhibited by feelings of failure as a result of these venial sins.

2. If mortal sin is rejection of love resulting in a total breach with God, venial sin is a refusal to love which weakens, but does not break, our relations with God. In venial sin we remain in a state of grace, the life of Christ is still in us, we are still temples of the Holy Spirit. We are still, therefore, 'pleasing to God', men who, in the words of the old version of the *Gloria*, are God's friends. But we have obscured and weakened that friendship. There is a helpful parallel in the case of a boy who has disobeyed his father. He knows his father will not drive him out of the house or cease to treat him as his son, but the bond between them has been weakened. Through venial sin we become, in Luther's words, though not his understanding of them, 'at once just and sinners'.

3. Theologians are not agreed on this point, but to my mind all refusal to respond to the demands of love is a sin—generally a venial sin. In other words all moral imperfection (in so far as it is deliberate) is sinful. If so, we all sin many times a day.

4. The Saints often described themselves as sinners. This was not an empty convention, nor the result of a morbidly sensitive conscience. The more one grows in the love of God, the more one becomes aware of the demands of love and of one's failure to respond to them. The prayer which Jesus praised was that of the Publican: 'God, be merciful to me a sinner' (Lk 18:13).

5.   We should therefore be impressed by the thought of our many sins. But not depressed. Depression comes from the urge to seek a sense of security from our own achievements–as sinners we can gain little comfort here. But what we must trust is the grace Christ has won for us on the cross. 'In you, Lord, we put our trust: we shall not be put to shame' (*Te Deum*).

6.   Grace includes forgiveness–we trust in the unfailing forgiveness of God. Human forgiveness tires when the fault is continually repeated; understandably, because true reconciliation requires action from both sides. But God's forgiveness never tires, provided there is repentance. The Good Shepherd never ceases to go out looking for his constantly wandering sheep. This is not softness in God; God is anything but soft; he is uncompromising in his insistence on what his love wills for us. Look at Lk 15.

7.   Grace is also healing. God does not only have to tend old wounds that constantly reopen. There will always be wounds, and they may always *seem* the same; but often we have grown, and our sins are now failures on a higher level of personal growth. We are now a different person, called to make a response to a situation which is now changed. We never swim in the same river twice, for the water has flowed on.

8.   The fruit of this meditation then is acceptance and trust. Acceptance of my sinfulness; trust in God.

9.   Sometimes we may feel an undefined sense of guilt. We feel we are not responding as we ought to the demands of love, but we cannot define exactly the point at which we have gone wrong. It is perhaps useless to try to define it; the need is still for acceptance–of my sinfulness, even if I may not be aware of sin on this particular occasion–and for trust in God's grace. Depression is an emotion which cannot always be controlled. But to give in

to it is always wrong: to do so is selfish (for it involves seeking to place our trust in ourselves) and lacking in trust of God.

10.   The undefined sense of guilt may be connected with the *present:* it may be an awareness that there are certain things we intend to hold on to, not because this is God's will, but because we want them. It is not certain they are not God's will: it may simply be that we dare not, or are not generous enough to, consider the matter with open minds. Sometimes the undefined sense of guilt is connected with the *past:* it may be the knowledge that we have been a contributory cause of harm (e.g. a quarrel, some failure by someone for whom we are responsible), and we cannot assess the extent of our culpability–if indeed there is any at all. The guilt-feeling about the present which I have described is different in two ways. First, it springs from an identifiable moral failure on our part; secondly, this failure is a persisting fact, not a thing of the past. We must seek God's pardon; and either take the hurdles we have so far refused, by seriously seeking God's will in the matter, or else confess to God our lack of generosity in refusing to consider his will. The fatal thing is to refuse to admit culpability, or to try to take some token action to appease our consciences, without seriously trying to find out God's will. We will remain spiritual dwarfs unless we are honest with ourselves and God.

11.   It is not much to trust in God's power to work in me if I raise no obstacles. What I need is trust in his power to work in me *despite* the obstacles I raise.

From the Spiritual Exercises of St Ignatius:

A particular examination, which involves three moments during the day, and requires us to examine ourselves twice daily.

The first moment is the morning, when, as soon as we waken, we should resolve to keep an attentive watch on some particular sin or vice we wish to correct (n. 24).

The second moment is the afternoon, when we ought to ask God for the grace to be able to recall how often we have fallen into this particular sin or fault, and the grace to correct ourselves in the future. After this we should make a first examination, calling ourselves to account with regard to the sin or defect in question, recalling each part of the day that has passed from our waking to the present moment, asking ourselves how many times we have committed the fault, and noting the number of times on a kind of graph. We should then resolve once more to control ourselves for the remainder of the day (n.25).

The third moment is after the evening meal, when we make a second examination, reviewing in the same way each hour that has passed between the preceding examination and the present moment. Having recalled in the same way the number of times we have failed, we should make a corresponding mark at the next point on the graph (n.26).

Each time we commit a sin or fault of this kind, we should express our regret by laying our hand on our breast. We can do this even in the presence of others without their noticing (n.27).

A GENERAL EXAMINATION OF CONSCIENCE[1] CONSISTING OF FIVE POINTS.

The first point is to give thanks to the lord our God for the benefits we have received from him.

The second point is to ask him for the grace to recognize our sins and to get rid of them.

The third point is to require of our soul an account of the sins committed during the present day, examining each hour since the time of rising: first faults of thought, then of word and of deed . . .

1. N.B. Many modern writers prefer to speak of an examination of *consciousness*. By this they mean that we should examine not only our faults, but also the way in which God has been guiding

us during the day, teaching us more about ourselves and facing us with new challenges.

The fourth point is to ask pardon of our Lord God for the faults we have committed.

The fifth point is to resolve with the grace of God to amend our lives.

We conclude with the Our Father (n.43).

RULES FOR THE DISCERNMENT OF SPIRITS

Some rules for recognizing the movements which arise in the soul so that one may consent only to those which are good and reject those which are evil (n.313).

1.   *To those who easily proceed from mortal sin to mortal sin, our enemy is accustomed to propose to the imagination specious pleasures and sensual delights, so as to confirm and even increase their sins and vices. The good spirit adopts the opposite mode of action, continually pricking their conscience, and appealing to their moral sense (n.314).*

2.   *When people try seriously to rid themselves of their sins and to advance in the service of God, the opposite is true: the evil spirit creates anxiety and gloom in their mind, and disturbs the soul with false reasons which impede its progress. By contrast it is characteristic of the good spirit to give greater courage and strength, to inspire tears of devotion, to enlighten the soul, to give peace and to remove all obstacles, so that one can make progress in virtue (n.315).*

Discipline

Throw away Thy rod,
Throw away Thy wrath;
O my God,
Take the gentle path.

For my heart's desire
Unto Thine is bent;
        I aspire
To a full consent.

Not a word or look
I affect to own,
        But by book,
And Thy Book alone.

Though I fail, I weep;
Though I halt in pace,
        Yet I creep
To the throne of grace.

Then let wrath remove;
Love will do the deed;
        For with love
Stony hearts will bleed.

Love is swift of foot;
Love's a man of war,
        And can shoot,
And can hit from far.

Who can 'scape his bow?
That which wrought on Thee,
        Brought Thee low,
Needs must work on me.

Throw away Thy rod:
Though man frailties hath,
        Thou art God;
Throw away Thy wrath.

GEORGE HERBERT

INTERLUDE 1: PRAYER

This interlude does not contain 'points for meditation'. It puts forward some ideas about prayer, and might helpfully be read at any time during the retreat; perhaps earlier rather than later.

The most important thing to grasp about prayer is that we need to pray. The Gospels show us our Lord frequently having recourse to prayer; after his baptism (Lk 3:21); before deciding to leave Capernaum (Mk 1:35); before calling the Twelve (Lk 6:12); after the feeding of the five thousand (Mk 6:46); before St Peter's profession of faith (Lk 9:18); at the Transfiguration (Lk 9:28–9); before teaching the Twelve the Lord's Prayer (Lk 11:1); at the Agony in the Garden; on the cross.

Why did he pray? Surely not simply to give us a good example. He did not just go through the motions of being a human being; he was a real man with real human needs. If he prayed, it was because he needed to pray–and for two reasons. First, prayer is the fulfilment of a human being's duty to adore his creator. Secondly, prayer is a source of strength and enlightenment; most of the occasions when the Gospels describe our Lord at prayer are moments when he is faced with a decision or a crisis. If Jesus needed to pray, so do we. Several of the passages suggest that Jesus' prayer was prolonged and deep. If we are to grow in the love of God and fulfil the destiny for which he made us, we too shall need to pray, not in a perfunctory or haphazard or spasmodic way, but purposefully. We need to *give* ourselves to prayer; to *want* to pray so keenly that we are willing to drop other concerns and habits which get in the way of our prayer. 'Pray without ceasing' (1 Thess 5:17). Am I allowing God to give me the depth of prayer that he wishes to give?

'No one can say "Jesus is Lord" except by the Holy Spirit' (1 Cor 12:3). Prayer is not a *natural* activity; we can pray only by God's grace. But to one in whom the Holy Spirit dwells, giving grace, prayer is what some theologians call *connatural*, meaning that the Holy Spirit makes us into the sort of beings who can pray. 'When we cry, "Abba! Father!" it is the Spirit himself bearing witness with our spirit that we are children of God' (Rom 8:16; cf. 8:26). We are able to pray, not simply because we are human beings, but because we are human beings transformed by the Holy Spirit, filled with grace.

That verse just quoted from Romans tells us more about prayer. Prayer is not only the gift of the Holy Spirit; it enables us to address God as our Father. We should not think that when we say the Lord's Prayer we call him our Father simply because he is our creator. As we are reminded by the words at Mass in which the priest invites the congregation to say the Lord's Prayer, to address God as our Father would be an act of extravagant presumption, if we did not have Jesus' prompting to do so. Again, when we call God our Father, we are bold enough to use the intimate form of address, 'Abba', which our Lord himself used in Gethsemane. When we pray, we act as members of God's family circle, the Blessed Trinity, speaking to our heavenly Father with the same familiarity as Jesus our Brother did, because we have been given a new life by the Holy Spirit, whom St Paul calls 'the Spirit of adoption'.

We are told to pray without ceasing. This clearly cannot mean that we are continually trying to put aside all other concerns in order to focus our entire loving attention on God. If we did that, the ordinary business of living would never get done. However, if the essence of prayer is the movement of the heart and will towards God, there is a sense in which we can pray more and more. An immature human being is one whose activities and desires are not integrated; there is little connection between his life at work, his life at home, and his life on the golf-course; there is no co-ordination in his life, to make all these activities exercises of a single master-drive. But if a man is a whole, and his wholeness consists in the fact that he is trying to love God with all his heart, soul, mind and strength, then the current that gives the power to all his activities in his love of God. To the extent to which that is true, he is seeking God always, and therefore praying always. 'To work is to pray.' But he will not be able to do this, unless there are the regular periods of deep recollection devoted to explicit prayer, with the attempt to put God in the centre of his consciousness. In the words of J. Dalrymple, both explicit prayer and Christian living are the 'affirmation' of Christ, by which we say 'yes' to his loving demands; but we will not say 'yes' consistently in our lives unless we say that 'yes' formally in our prayers. To work is to pray only if regularly we pray without working.

All of this is summed up in the traditional definition of prayer as 'the raising of the mind and heart to God.' Mind *and heart*. Prayer is not just thought about God, but is personal contact with our Father, in union with his Son, our Brother, through the gift of the Holy Spirit. Therefore thoughts articulated into words are not essential to prayer; there can be prayer without words, but there cannot be prayer without this person-to-person contact which we call a movement of the heart or the will. Nevertheless we first learn to pray in fixed forms of words, which most of us learn in the home, at school and in church. Then we discover that we can talk to God in our own words, and in forms of group prayer we may share this more spontaneous prayer with others. But even in public worship we soon learn (though often without adverting to the fact) that there is more to prayer than words; music helps us to put more of our hearts into our forms of words; and ceremonies and symbols, like offertory processions, candles and incense, can be means of reinforcing the thoughts that we express in words. We may learn too that listening to the word of God or reading it is a form of prayer, involving a loving attention to God; though we may feel the need to focus our response in words. But gradually we may come to experience the value of silence in prayer: not just of spoken words, but doing without words even in our hearts. Our prayer comes to consist of a rhythm of words and silence. We may find the words becoming fewer and fewer, and the periods of silence becoming greater, so that the words serve simply to relieve tension or to provide some rhythm, perhaps a very slow rhythm, to our wordless prayer. Some people follow the rhythm of breathing. Many people find it helpful to use the same phrase over and over again, probably some pregnant phrase from scripture, like 'My Lord and my God', 'Help my unbelief', 'Lord, if you will, you can make me clean.' Others, who have more pictorial imaginations, may find themselves helped by an image held in the mind's eye, or even by some gesture, whether real (such as kneeling) or imagined (such as feeling as if one were stretching out one's hands in supplication). But it becomes clearer and clearer that the essence of the prayer is the wordless movement of the heart.

From the Spiritual Exercises of St Ignatius:

Second Method of Prayer, *by directing the attention to the meaning of each of the words of the prayer (n.249).*

In the Second Method of Prayer we should kneel or sit, according to the condition of the body and interior devotion, and shut our eyes or fix them on a particular point without letting them wander. [We should then recite the Lord's Prayer]. At the first word 'Father'[1] we pause to meditate as long as we find in it meanings, analogies, spiritual 'taste' and consolation. We do the same for each word of the Our Father or of some other prayer. (n.252).

Third Method of Prayer, *which is rhythmical. With each breath we pray mentally, repeating one of the words of the Lord's Prayer or of another prayer, so that only one word is said between one breath and the next. In the space between breaths we should concentrate on the meaning of the word, or on the person to whom the prayer is addressed, or our own unworthiness, or the difference between us. We should then proceed in the same way with regard to the remaining words of the Our Father, and of other prayers (n.258).*

1 In Latin the first word of the Lord's Prayer is 'Pater' (Father). Those who pray in English could of course begin with the word 'Our'.

PART TWO: THE FOLLOWING OF CHRIST

8. THE VOCATION OF CHRISTIANS

1. So far we have been turning over in our minds the implications of the fact that God is our Creator and our Father. Now we consider a new factor in our relationship with God. He has not only made us: he has called us. All Christians are called by God; among them some are called to the life of religious or priests. In this meditation we ask for the grace to respond generously to God's call to be Christians.

2. In the Old Testament there is a recurrent pattern in the way God's call comes to the prophets. In Jer 1:3–10 the following elements of the pattern are discernible:
(a) God's word comes at a particular moment (vv.3, 10).
(b) God tells the prophet he was planned from the first moment of his existence for his destiny to be a prophet (v.5).
(c) This destiny involves a special intimacy with God: 'I knew you . . . I consecrated you' (v.5).
(d) The prophet expresses diffidence: 'Ah Lord God! Behold! I do not know how to speak, for I am only a youth' (v.6).
(e) Resistance is useless, fears groundless, because the authority of God is unquestionable: 'To all to whom I send you you shall go, and whatever I command you you shall speak' (v.7).
(f) A symbolic, almost sacramental, act by which God empowers the prophet; here he puts forth his hand and touches Jeremiah's lips: 'Behold, I have put my words in your mouth' (v.9).

3. There are other examples, in the commissioning of Isaiah

(6:1–9), and, at greater length, of Moses (Ex 3:1–4:17). The same features are evident in the satirical account of Jonah's call. Second Isaiah also applies the idea of the call to the whole people: 'Fear not, for I have redeemed you. I have called you by name, you are mine' (43:1).

4.   The New Testament writers apply this idea of a call to the Christian: 'He chose us in him [Christ] before the foundation of the world, that we should be holy [*hagious*, dedicated] and blameless before him. He destined us in love to be his sons thorough Jesus Christ' (Eph 1:4–5).

> 'God is faithful, by whom you were called into the fellowship of his Son, Jesus Christ our Lord' (1 Cor 1:9).
> Suffer in silence when wrongly blamed: 'For to this you have been called, because Christ also suffered for you, leaving you an example, that you should follow in his steps' (1 Pet 2:21).
> The Good Shepherd calls his sheep by name (Jn 10:3).

5.   From these passages it follows:
(a) We are called, chosen. This implies a special purpose for which we were created.
(b) God empowers us for following the call.
(c) We are called in Christ, into fellowship with him, to follow his example, e.g. in accepting blame.
(d) The call involves dedication to God, holiness.
(e) God commits himself to helping us, and he is 'faithful'.
(f) It is an individual call, with an individual destiny for each: 'To him who conquers I will give some of the hidden manna, and I will give him a white stone, with a new name written on the stone which no one knows except him who receives it' (Rev 2:17).

6.   It is a call, an invitation, which requires a free, not a coerced response. God treats his creatures with respect. Although acceptance of the call will involve us in *working for* Christ, essential to

the call is the invitation to be *with* him. What Christ wants is not so much our work, as ourselves.

7. What should our response be like? 'Strive to enter by the narrow door' (Lk 13:24). 'The kingdom of heaven has suffered violence, and men of violence take it by force' (Mt 11:12). 'The kingdom of heaven is like treasure hidden in a field . . . *In his joy* he goes and sells all he has . . . The kingdom of heaven is like a merchant in search of fine pearls, who, on finding one pearl of great value, went and sold all that he had and bought it' (Mt 13:44–6). '"Are you able to drink the cup that I am to drink?" . . . "We are able"' (Mt 20:22). We must not be like the rich young man whom Jesus 'looked upon and loved', but who 'went away sorrowful' because he could not bear to follow Jesus at the cost of selling all (Mk 10:21–2).

The Hound of Heaven

I fled Him, down the nights and down the days;
   I fled Him, down the arches of the years;
I fled Him, down the labyrinthine ways
   Of my own mind; and in the mist of tears
I hid from Him, and under running laughter.
      Up vistaed hopes I sped;
      And shot, precipitated,
Adown Titanic glooms of chasmèd fears,
   From those strong Feet that followed, followed after.

      But with unhurrying chase,
      And unperturbèd pace,
Deliberate speed, majestic instancy.
      They beat—and a Voice beat
      More instant than the Feet—
"All things betray thee, who betrayest Me."

FRANCIS THOMPSON

9. THE CALL OF
THE APOSTLES

1. In this meditation we take one particular aspect of the Christian vocation which we considered last time: our call to be apostles. This is a call which is given, a duty which is placed, on every Christian. A Christian is a man or woman for others. When we are confirmed (confirmation is one of the final stages in our initiation as Christians) we receive the Holy Spirit to make us, like the Apostles at Pentecost, witnesses of Christ. Our Lord's words, 'As the Father has sent me, even so I send you ... Receive the Holy Spirit' (Jn 20:21–2), though addressed to the Apostles, apply to every Christian. (Some, however, are called to a particular state of life, especially the religious life of the vows, in which, being detached from family ties, they are able to devote themselves more fully to the vocation which they share with all Christians.) The grace therefore that we seek is that we may be generous in accepting Christ's invitation to follow him in proclaiming the Gospel.

2. Like the prophets, the Apostles also were called, but there is an added dimension to their call. They were called not only to perform a particular work, but to follow Christ.

'And passing along by the Sea of Galilee, he saw Simon and Andrew the brother of Simon casting a net in the sea; for they were fishermen. And Jesus said to them, "Follow me and I will make you become fishers of men." And immediately they left their nets and followed him' (Mk 1:16–8).

'As Jesus passed on from there, he saw a man called Matthew sitting at the tax office; and he said to him, "Follow me." And he rose and followed him' (Mt 9:9).

'But when Simon Peter saw it [the miraculous catch of fish], he fell down at Jesus' knees, saying, "Depart from me, for I am a sinful man, O Lord." . . . And Jesus said to Simon, "Do not be afraid; henceforth you will be catching men." And when they had brought their boats to land, they left everything and followed him' (Lk 5:8–11). Peter, like the prophets, is initially reluctant to accept the call.

John the Baptist 'looked at Jesus as he walked, and said, "Behold, the Lamb of God!" The two disciples heard him say this, and they followed Jesus. Jesus turned, and saw them following, and said to them, "What do you seek?" And they said to him, "Rabbi, . . . where are you staying?" He said to them, "Come and see." They came and saw where he was staying; and they stayed with him that day' (Jn 1:36–9).

'The next day Jesus decided to go to Galilee. And he found Philip and said to him, "Follow me."' (Jn 1:43).

This last quotation contains the point in a nutshell. Jesus *finds* us. He is attracting us like a magnet, if only we will let go.

3. They are called to follow Jesus, and to be fishers for human beings. We see the same two aspects of an apostolic vocation when Jesus solemnly picks out the Twelve from the other disciples. 'And he went up into the hills, and called to him *those whom he desired*; and they came to him. And he appointed twelve, to be with him, and to be sent out to preach and have authority to cast out demons' (Mk 3:13–5). There can be no spiritual power in an apostolic life that concentrates on the second aspect at the expense of the first.

4. When we read the account of the call of St Paul in Acts, we see a third strand: the call to suffer for Christ. Acts gives three accounts of the episode: 9:1–19; 22:4–16; 26:9–18. On the way to Damascus, where he is intending to persecute the Christians in his zeal for the Jewish law, having asked the High Priest for letters of authorization, 'suddenly a light from heaven flashed about him. And he fell to the ground and heard a voice saying to

c

him, "Saul, Saul, why do you persecute me?"' (9:3–4). '"It hurts you to kick against the goads"' (26:14). '"Who are you, Lord?" And he said, "I am Jesus, whom you are persecuting"' (9:5). '"What shall I do, Lord?"' (22:10). '"Rise and stand upon your feet; for I have appeared to you for this purpose, to appoint you to serve and bear witness to the things in which you have seen me and to those in which I will appear to you, delivering you from the people and from the Gentiles–to whom I send you to open their eyes"' (26:16–18). Saul was led into Damascus, unable to see because of the brightness of that light (cf. 22:11). In Damascus Ananias had a vision of the Lord preparing him to restore Saul's sight. '"He is a chosen instrument of mine to carry my name before the Gentiles and kings and the sons of Israel; for I will show him *how much he must suffer for the sake of my name*"' (9:15–16).

5.   The principles concerning the apostolate which are apparent in the conversion of Paul are valid also for our own calling. The apostolate to which we are all called involves:

(a)   Being chosen. Though we are not dragooned, but are invited to make a free response, nevertheless the initiative is not ours. 'You did not choose me, but I chose you' (Jn 15:16).

(b)   Being witnesses to what we have seen. But if we have not become familiar with Christ by deep prayer, we cannot be witnesses to what we have not seen. Our witness will not be valid, if all we can give is hearsay evidence.

(c)   Christ's call is insistent. He will keep knocking. We can pretend not to hear, but it will 'hurt' us.

(d)   The enterprise is of a daunting magnitude, but 'I will appear to you, delivering you.' 'Rise and stand upon your feet.'

(e)   Success in Christ's service is bound up with suffering for the sake of his name.

(f)   First and last, it is a call to be with Jesus.

From the Spiritual Exercises of St Ignatius:

CONTEMPLATION OF THE KINGDOM OF JESUS CHRIST

The call of an earthly king helps us to contemplate the life of the Eternal King.

The first preparatory prayer is the same as before [cf. p.42]

The first prelude, the composition of place, is to see in the imagination the synagogues, villages and towns which Christ our Lord passed through as he was preaching.

The second prelude consists in asking for the grace which I desire. Here it will be to ask our Lord for the grace that I may not be deaf to his call, but prompt and diligent to fulfil his most holy will (n.91).

The first point is to set before my eyes a human king, chosen by our Lord God, to whom all the princes and people of Christendom owe reverence and obedience (n.92).

The second point is to observe how the king addresses all his subjects as follows: 'It is my wish to conquer all the lands of the infidels. Anyone who wishes to accompany me must be prepared to have the same food, drink, clothes and other things which he will see that I have; he will have to toil as I do by day, and watch by night, etc., so that a man will share in my victory to the extent to which he shares my labours' (n.93).

The third point is to consider the reply which faithful subjects will make to so generous and kind a king. Consequently if anyone refuses the request of such a king he will deserve everyone's contempt and be reckoned a cowardly knight (n.94).

67

The second part of this exercise consists of drawing a comparison between the earthly king and our Lord. There will be three points.

First, if the earthly king, when he calls his subjects, deserves our respect, how much more is this true of Christ our Lord, the eternal and glorious King as he addresses the world as a whole and each person individually in these words: 'It is my will to conquer the whole world and all my enemies, and so to enter into the glory of my Father. Accordingly anyone who wishes to come with me must toil with me, so that, following me in hardship, he may follow me also in glory' (n.95).

Secondly, we will reflect that no one of sound instincts and good sense will refuse to offer himself wholeheartedly for the work (n.96).

Thirdly, we should judge that those who wish to show greater devotion and to distinguish themselves in unstinting service of their eternal King and Lord of all, will not only offer themselves for toil, but will make offerings of greater worth and distinction, going against their love of bodily ease and worldly desires, in words like these (n.97):

'Eternal Lord of all things, trusting in your grace and your help, I make my offering in the presence of your infinite goodness, and of your glorious Mother and of all the men and women saints in your heavenly court. I declare that I wish and desire and determine with full deliberation to imitate you in bearing every kind of contempt and insult, and in bearing true poverty, both spiritual and even material, provided this contributes more to your service and praise, and if it pleases your Sacred Majesty to choose and admit me to such a state of life' (n.98).

The Lantern Out of Doors

Sometimes a lantern moves along the night,
    That interests our eyes. And who goes there?
    I think; where from and bound, I wonder, where,
With, all down darkness wide, his wading light?

Men go by me whom either beauty bright
  In mould or mind or what not else makes rare:
  They rain against our much–thick and marsh air
Rich beams, till death or distance buys them quite.

Death or distance soon consumes them: wind
  What most I may eye after, be in at the end
I cannot, and out of sight is out of mind.

Christ minds; Christ's interest, what to avow or amend
  There, éyes them, heart wánts, care haúnts, foot fóllows kínd,
Their ránsom, théir rescue, ánd first, fást, last friénd.

GERARD MANLEY HOPKINS

10. THE INCARNATION

1. We have been praying in the last two sections about our vocation to follow Christ. For the rest of this retreat the following of Christ is the keynote of our prayer. We are called to follow him not only by co-operating in his work of saving the world, by obeying his commands and imitating him; we are called to make his mind and heart our own, to share his attitudes, his values. 'Have this mind among yourselves, which was in Christ Jesus' (Phil 2:5). 'Put on the Lord Jesus Christ' (Rom 13:14). If we do not try to do this, we shall just be going through the motions of responding to his call. The grace therefore that we ask for is expressed in the prayer of St Richard of Chichester: 'O most merciful Redeemer, Friend and Brother, may I know thee more clearly, love thee more dearly, and follow thee more nearly'. (Some may recall the setting of these words in the musical play *Godspell*.)

2. At this point in the retreat, then, we begin to do two things. The first is to put before our minds the life of Jesus, praying that we may learn from him, for he is gentle and lowly in heart (cf. Mt 11:29; some commentators think our Lord is referring to himself as Wisdom, as in Sir (Ecclesiasticus) 24:19; 51:23–7). The second aim we have is to begin to consider any decision we may have to make (see Introduction, p.15), for the more important a decision, the more it needs to be taken according to Christ's values. In this particular meditation we hold the Incarnation itself before our eyes, in order that Christ's values may penetrate us, attract us, influence us. If anyone finds this section heavy and theological, they might like to begin with paragraph 7.

3.   'The Word became flesh' (Jn 1:14). Why? The first reason is to be a revelation to us. This seems to be one of the ideas John has in mind when he calls Christ 'The Word'. To understand this term fully we would have to study the Old Testament and the Greek philosophers, for it has a specialized meaning in both these sources. But whatever else John means by it, 'the Word' certainly means for him the self-expression of God. What does a word mean for us? We put our thoughts in words, in our own minds, and when we speak to our friends; so, unless we are engaging in a pretence, or unless we speak the merest trivialities, our words allow our listeners to peep in at a window and see something of ourselves. Our words are images of ourselves. So from all eternity the Word is the image of God the Father, though there was no one but God to contemplate it; God speaks his Word to himself. But once he created human beings, he had an audience, and spoke his Word revealing his secret to them. He was not content to reveal himself in his creation, as a draftsman reveals himself in his handiwork, or as anyone reveals himself by talking about himself. God revealed himself again in a new way when his Word became a human being, so that everything that man Jesus said and did and had done to him revealed God, because it is God himself saying and doing and being done to. 'No one has ever seen God,' St John went on; 'the only Son, who is in the bosom of the Father, he has made him known' (Jn 1:18). In other words, Jesus 'reflects the glory of God, and bears the very stamp of his nature' (Heb 1:3); 'he is the image of the invisible God' (Col 1:15). 'He who has seen me has seen the Father' (Jn 14:9). Everything in Jesus' life belongs to the Word, and the Word exists only as the self-expression of the Father. We contemplate Jesus' life, then, in order to understand God.

4.   The Word also reveals to us God's loving plan for human beings. Jesus is God's Wisdom, that is to say, God's wisdom concerning human life. 'Learn from me . . ., and you will find

rest for your souls. For my yoke is easy, and my burden is light'
(Mt 11:29-30). God's will for us is not an arbitrary imposition; it
is the law of our nature. 'This commandment which I command
you this day is not too hard for you, neither is it far off . . . The
Word is very near you; it is in your mouth and in your heart'
(Deut 30:11,14). Jesus shares our nature, and is therefore subject
to the same law. Everything in his life reveals that commandment to us; he *is* the Word conveying God's plan to us; for 'my
food is to do the will of him who sent me' (Jn 4:34).

5.   There is a second reason why the Word became flesh: to
redeem us. We should recall our thoughts of the first part of the
retreat, when we were thinking of our sins and our need of
redemption. We should let our minds dwell on this great fact,
that the life and death of this one man redeemed the whole
world. There are many ways in which the New Testament
writers expressed this truth.

(a) The fundamental notion is that Jesus catches us up into
his own life of complete dedication to his Father. In the phrase
that St Paul uses so often, we become 'in Christ', the parts of his
body. Speaking of spiritual more than physical death, he writes,
'As in Adam all die, so also in Christ shall all be made alive' (1
Cor 15:22). As Adam was thought in his sin to represent the
whole human race, so Christ, who 'sums up' (or 'unites': cf. Eph
1:10) and restores it by his goodness, is the second or last Adam
(1 Cor 15:45).

(b) He redeems us by teaching us, as we have just seen: 'I am
the light of the world' (Jn 8:12).

(c) He redeems us by overcoming the forces of evil: 'Since
therefore the children share in flesh and blood, he himself
likewise partook of the same nature, that through death he might
destroy him who has the power of death, that is the devil, and
deliver all those who through fear of death were subject to
lifelong bondage' (Heb 2:14–15).

(d) He redeems us by effecting a reconciliation–not so much reconciling God the Father to us (it is only because God had *already* been merciful that the Saviour came into the world) as reconciling us to God: 'God was in Christ reconciling the world to himself' (2 Cor 5:19). 'There is one mediator between God and men, the man Christ Jesus' (1 Tim 2:5).

(e) He redeems us by offering himself as a sacrifice on our behalf to his Father. 'Christ loved us and gave himself up for us, a fragrant offering and sacrifice to God' (Eph 5:2). The sacrifice Jesus offered to his Father on our behalf was not his pain or his death in themselves (for they could give a loving Father no pleasure), but his obedience. Hebrews connects the Incarnation with Psalm 40: 'When Christ came into the world, he said, "Sacrifices and offerings thou hast not desired, but a body thou hast prepared for me; in burnt offerings and sin offerings thou hast taken no pleasure. Then I said, 'Lo, I have come to do thy will, O God,' as it is written of me in the roll of the book"' (10:5–7). Indeed St John seems to regard the Father not as the one who receives his Son's sacrifice but rather as the Father who sacrifices his only Son, as Abraham was prepared to sacrifice Isaac: 'God loved the world so much that he gave his only Son' (3:16).

6.   There is a third reason why God the Son became man: he wished to be one of us. In this sense Matthew applied to the conception of Jesus Isaiah's prophecy: '"Behold, a virgin shall conceive and bear a son, and his name shall be called Emmanuel" (which means, God with us)' (1:23). 'For we have not a high priest who is unable to sympathize with us in our weaknesses, but one who in every respect has been tempted as we are, yet without sinning' (Heb 4:15). The most cogent answer to the question why God allows people to suffer is to say that he became one of us and suffers with us. Moreover, as the Fathers of the early Church saw so clearly, it was by coming down to our level that God was able to raise us up to his level: God became man so that man might be (bold paradox) deified. As the priest prays silently at the Offertory of the Mass: 'May we come to

share in the divinity of Christ, who humbled himself to share in our humanity.'

7.   With these thoughts in our minds let us turn to the moment of the Incarnation. The angel tells a young girl: 'You will conceive in your womb and bear a son . . . He will be great, and will be called the Son of the Most High.' 'I am the handmaid of the Lord' she replies; 'let it be to me according to your word' (Lk 1:31–8). 'And the Word became flesh and dwelt among us' (Jn 1:14).

8.   This is an appropriate point for the retreatant to consider another kind of prayer besides the word-based methods described on pp.13,58. This new method consists of relating ourselves more imaginatively to a gospel scene. After the usual prayer for the grace to pray and for the grace of this particular stage in the retreat, we can proceed in two ways. The first is to reflect on the significance of the incident: who is there? what are they doing? what are they saying? what are they feeling? why are they doing this? why is this important for me? This is the method which Ignatius outlines in the meditation on the Incarnation (pp.75–77), in which he asks us to reflect on the persons, their words and their actions 'so that we may derive some fruit from the scene'. The second method engages the heart more than the head: Ignatius calls it the Application of the Senses (p.83). We try to feel what it was like to be there. It doesn't matter if our guesses are all wrong; for these purposes whatever we feel is right. We *see* the room where Mary is praying when Gabriel suddenly appears, see the majesty or the simplicity of the angel. We *hear* his voice, awe-inspiring or calming. We *smell* the domestic smells of Mary's house, the scent of the fields outside, perhaps the sacred perfume of the angel's clothes. We *touch* the seat where Mary is sitting, the hem of her robe, the angel's feet. We *feel* the room, warm in the heat of a Palestine spring, perhaps the thrill of fear at the sight of the angel, the racing of the pulse,

the beating of the heart. We feel ourselves part of the scene: where are we, at Mary's side, at the angel's, looking on apart, sensing deeply our need for the Saviour and longing for Mary to say yes? But we must make sure this is prayer and not daydreaming: though we may not be reasoning or formulating prayers in our minds, we need to feel our connection with the scene in our hearts. And we should conclude by expressing our reactions to one or more of the people who took part in the scene, and then reciting a familiar prayer like the Our Father or (most appropriate to this incident) the Hail Mary.

From the Spiritual Exercises of St Ignatius:

THE INCARNATION OF JESUS CHRIST

This meditation consists of the preparatory prayer, three preludes and three points with a colloquy.

The preparatory prayer is as before (n.101).

The first prelude is to recall the facts. Here it is how the three divine persons, observing the earth teeming with human beings all on the way to hell, decide from all eternity that the Second Person shall assume the nature of a man for the salvation of the human race. And so, when the fullness of time had come,[1] the angel St Gabriel is sent as a messenger to our Lady (n.102).

The second prelude is the composition of place. Here it consists of seeing in the imagination the great globe inhabited by so many diverse races. Then one will envisage one particular spot on the earth, the rooms of our Lady's house at Nazareth in the province of Galilee (n.103).

The third prelude is to ask for what I desire, namely an intimate knowledge

1 Gal 4.4.

of the Lord who became man for my sake, so that I may better love him and follow him (n.104).

N.B.   The preparatory prayer and the three preludes are made in the same way throughout this part and for the rest of the retreat, with adjustments according to the subject-matter (n.105).

The first point is to note all the persons *involved. First, the human beings living on the face of the earth, so different in their dress and their customs; some white and others black, some in peace, others at war; some weeping, others laughing; some in good health, others in bad; some being born, and others dying; etc.*

Then one should contemplate the three divine persons looking down from the royal throne of their majesty on the whole face of the earth, and on all the races there in their blindness, as they die and go to hell.

Finally we contemplate our Lady and the angel who greets her, always relating what we see to ourselves, so that we may derive some fruit from the scene (n.106).

The second point is to hear what each of the persons is saying: *the human beings on earth speaking among themselves, swearing and blaspheming; the divine persons saying, 'Let us bring about the redemption of the human race'; our Lady and the angel conversing together. I reflect on all this so as to gather fruit from these words (n.107).*

The third point will be to attend similarly to the actions *of the persons: how the human beings are striking and killing one another, and going to hell; how the divine persons are bringing about the most holy Incarnation; how the angel fulfils his mission as ambassador, and our Lady behaves most humbly and pays thanks to the divine Majesty. Then we reflect so as to gather fruit from each of these things (n.108).*

Finally, I add a colloquy, asking myself what I ought to say to each of the divine persons, to the eternal Word made man, or to his mother our Lady, asking them, as I feel drawn, for everything that can help me better to follow and imitate my newly incarnate Lord. We conclude by reciting the Our Father (n.109).

From *The Wreck of the Deutschland*

Not out of his bliss
Springs the stress felt
Nor first from heaven (and few know this)
Swings the stroke dealt –
Stroke and a stress that stars and storms deliver,
That guilt is hushed by, hearts are flushed by and melt –
But it rides time like riding a river
(And here the faithful waver, the faithless fable and miss).

It dates from day
Of his going in Galilee;
Warm-laid grave of a womb-life grey;
Manger, maiden's knee;
The dense and the driven Passion, and frightful sweat;
Thence the discharge of it, there its swelling to be,
Though felt before, though in high flood yet –
What none would have known of it, only the heart, being hard
at bay,

Is out with it! Oh,
We lash with the best or worst
Word last! How a lush-kept plush-capped sloe
Will, mouthed to flesh-burst,
Gush! – flush the man, the being with it, sour or sweet,
Brim, in a flash, full! – Hither then, last or first,
To hero of Calvary, Christ's feet –
Never ask if meaning it, wanting it, warned of it – men go.

GERARD MANLEY HOPKINS

11. THE ANNUNCIATION

1. The grace for which we pray is that we may make our own Christ's values, which we can learn from St Luke's account of God the Son's entry into the world (Lk 1:26-38). We can see these values reflected in the person of his Mother. May we know him more clearly, love him more dearly and follow him more nearly in the mystery of the Annunciation.

2. Many commentators point out that St Luke regards Mary as the *representative of God's people* of the Old Testament waiting for the Messiah. The prophet Zechariah had addressed his prediction of a joyful future to a symbolic woman who stands for the whole people: 'Sing and rejoice, O daughter of Zion; for lo, I come and I will dwell in the midst of you, says the Lord' (Zech 2:10; cf. Zeph 3:14–6). Mary is the new daughter of Zion, who hears herself bidden by the angel: 'Rejoice [this is the literal meaning of "hail"] . . . The Lord is with you' (Lk 1:28). Mary is the neck of the hour-glass, where the Old Testament contracts into her person, and from her springs Christ, from whom the New Testament will spread out into the multitude of his followers. No other human beings, her Son apart, carried such a responsibility; God waits for her response before bringing about the Incarnation; on the single moment of her decision the destiny of mankind was poised trembling. And she is told to rejoice.

3. Gabriel addresses, the daughter of Zion as '*full of grace*' or 'highly favoured one'. The two translations, which seem so different, converge. God's grace or favour is never a capricious preference; it is creative; those whom God favours he fills with grace. 'As the rain and the snow come down from heaven, and return not thither but water the earth, making it bring forth and sprout, giving seed to the sower and bread to the eater, so shall my word be that goes forth from my mouth; it shall not return to

me empty, but it shall accomplish that which I purpose, and prosper in the things for which I sent it' (Is 55:10–11).

4.   She is 'a *virgin* betrothed' (Lk 1:27). When told she is to be the mother of 'the Son of the Most High' (1:32), her reply, literally translated, is: 'How can this be, since I have no knowledge of man [i.e. since I am still a virgin]?' (1:34). Her virginity will become fruitful because the Holy Spirit will come upon her, and the power of the Most High will overshadow her (1:35). The words recall the cloud and the light of glory which marked God's presence in the tabernacle when the Israelites were in the desert (Ex 40:34–8). God's creative power also brings life to Elizabeth's sterile womb; 'for with God nothing will be impossible' (1:37).

5.   She is the *obedient* virgin. 'Behold, I am the handmaid of the Lord; let it be to me according to your word' (1:38). Her obedience is also described as faith: 'Blessed is she who believed that there would be a fulfilment of what was spoken to her from the Lord' (1:45; cf. 11:28). In contrast, when the same angel Gabriel had anounced to Zechariah that his wife was to bear him a son in their old age, Zechariah had not believed and was condemned to dumbness, 'because you did not believe my words, which will be fulfilled in their time' (1:20).

6.   She is the *humble* virgin. Her *Magnificat* proclaims how the power of God is able to work in the humble: 'He has regarded the low estate of his handmaiden . . . He who is mighty has done great things for me . . . He has filled the hungry with good things, and the rich he has sent empty away' (1:48, 49, 53). The words suggest that her humility is not just a quality of mind, but an actual underprivileged condition. Was it her poverty? (When presenting her Son in the Temple she made the poor person's offering of a dove or a pigeon rather than a lamb: Lk 2:24; cf. Lev 12:8). Or was it a commitment to virginity?

7.   She is a *contemplative* virgin. We can imagine how her prayer and her joy centred on the treasure she was carrying in her womb. But her reflective inner silence is not left totally to our imaginations. Twice in almost identical words St Luke tells us that Mary 'kept' the words that she heard 'pondering them in her heart' (2:19; cf. 2:51). It was this contemplative familiarity with God and his word which had made her able to welcome the message that came from God and 'keep' it (cf. Lk 11:28). It was this same familiarity with God's purposes which would enable her to help her Son to grow 'in wisdom and in stature, and in favour with God and man' (2:52; cf. 2:40). Again, her insight into God's plan must have helped her Son at least in the first stages of his own growing understanding of his Father's will.

8.   'Blessed are you among women, and blessed is the fruit of your womb!' (Lk 1:42).

"Ave Maria Gratia Plena"

Was this His coming! I had hoped to see
A scene of wondrous glory, as was told
Of some great God who in a rain of gold
Broke open bars and fell on Danae:
Or a dread vision as when Semele,
Sickening for love and unappeased desire,
Prayed to see God's clear body, and the fire
Caught her brown limbs and slew her utterly.
With such glad dreams I sought this holy place,
And now with wondering eyes and heart I stand
Before this supreme mystery of Love:
Some kneeling girl with passionless pale face,
An angel with a lily in his hand,
And over both the white wings of a Dove.

OSCAR WILDE

12. THE NATIVITY

1. We pray for grace to know our Lord better, love him more and follow him more closely in his Nativity.

2. His coming brings *joy*. The shepherds were filled with fear, but they were told: 'Be not afraid; for behold, I bring you good news of a great joy which will come to all the people' (Lk 2:10). He always brings reassurance and joy. 'Peace to his people on earth': we borrow the angel's prayer, 'Glory to God in the highest' (2:14), for the Gloria of the Mass. The reason why the shepherds are told to rejoice is: 'To you is born this day in the city of David a Saviour, who is Christ the Lord' (2:11). A Saviour: we recall our meditations on sin and our need for salvation. Christ: the Messiah, the anointed one, anointed as our king, our priest and our Prophet. The Lord: God the Son, who wishes so much to bring us into contact with him that he becomes one of us.

3. 'The *glory* of the Lord shone around' the shepherds. The multitude of angels sang: 'Glory to God in the highest.' The glory is the brightness which marked God's presence in the Old Testament (Ex 40:34–8). It appeared over our Lord again at the Transfiguration (Lk 9:29–32). This new-born baby is the radiance of the Father's glory (Heb 1:3). His weakness conceals the infinite perfection of God. But it also *reveals* God's perfection. 'No one has ever seen God; the only Son, who is in the bosom of the Father, He has made him known' (Jn 1:18). What is there in God which, in terms of human existence, is best expressed as a baby in a manger? Is it that God is a self-sacrificing God?

4. The child is born in *weakness*, the weakness proper to a new-

born baby. He was not playing a game, going through the motions of being weak, while all the time restraining his infinite strength; pretending to be limited in his mind to the helpless explorations of an infant, while all the time his human mind was flooded with divine light. The Incarnation is 'for real'. Like any new-born child, Jesus is locked in the physical and psychological limitations of his age. 'Since therefore the children share in flesh and blood, he himself likewise partook of the same nature . . . Therefore he had to be made like his brethren in every respect . . . We have not a high priest who is unable to sympathize with our weaknesses' (Heb 2:14, 17; 4:15).

5.   He was also born into weakness in comparison with other babies. St Paul sees *poverty* as the note of the Incarnation: 'You know the grace of our Lord Jesus Christ, that though he was rich, yet for your sake he became poor, so that by his poverty you might become rich' (2 Cor 8:9). He was born in a stable; among the poor at his presentation in the Temple; a political refugee in Egypt; one whom the people of Nazareth thought as ordinary as themselves: '"Where did this man get all this? . . . Is not this the carpenter, the son of Mary and brother of James and Joses and Judas and Simon, and are not his sisters here with us?" And they took offence at him' (Mk 6:2–3). He lived in a despised town: 'Can anything good come out of Nazareth?' (Jn 1:46). He later lived the life of a wandering preacher, so that he could say: 'Foxes have holes, and birds of the air have nests; but the Son of Man has nowhere to lay his head' (Lk 9:58). Yet we should not exaggerate: Jesus did not live in destitution or near-starvation; the apostles had a common purse, and women at least some of the time looked after their needs (Mk 15:41). In the end, though, he was stripped of all, and died naked on the cross.

6.   What St Paul said of Jesus' self-emptying obedience applies also to his poverty: 'Have the mind among yourselves, which was in Christ Jesus' (Phil 2:5). If we truly share Christ's mind,

we will feel an affinity with the underprivileged and the outcasts; even the undeserving, repulsive poor. We will be concerned for social justice. May we understand his poverty, be attracted by it, and pray without pretence that, despite our fears and self-love, we may allow some share of it into our own lives.

From the Spiritual Exercises of St Ignatius:

APPLICATION OF THE SENSES

After the preparatory prayer and the three preludes indicated above, it is desirable where appropriate to apply the five senses of the imagination to the subject-matter of the preceding contemplations (n.121).

The first point will be in the imagination to see *all the persons, noting all the details, so as to gather fruit from what we see (n.122).*

The second point is to hear *what they are saying, or what it is appropriate for them to say, and to apply it all to our own situation (n.123).*

The third point is to employ, as it were, an interior sense of taste *or* smell, *so as to feel the infinite fragrance and sweetness of the divinity, or of a soul with its virtues, etc., having regard for the person whom we are considering, and to reflect inwardly and adapt whatever is profitable to our own case (n.124).*

The fourth point is to touch, *for example to handle and kiss, the places where these people are walking and sitting, always making sure that we derive some fruit from this (n.125).*

As before, we should conclude this contemplation with a colloquy, followed by the Our Father (n.126).

A Christmas Carol

Lacking samite and sable,
Lacking silver and gold,
The Prince Jesus in the poor stable
Slept, and was three hours old.

As doves by the fair water,
Mary, not touched of sin,
Sat by Him,—the King's daughter,
All glorious within.

A lily without one stain, a
Star where no spot hath room—
Ave, gratia plena,
Virgo Virginum.

Clad not in pearl-sewn vesture,
Clad not in cramoisie,
She hath hushed, she hath cradled to rest, her
God the first time on her knee.

Where is one to adore Him?
The ox hath dumbly confessed,
With the ass, meek kneeling before Him,
"Et homo factus est."

Not throned on ivory or cedar,
Not crowned with a Queen's crown,
At her breast it is Mary shall feed her
Maker, from Heaven come down.

The trees in Paradise blossom
Sudden, and its bells chime—
She giveth Him, held to her bosom,
Her immaculate milk the first time.

The night with wings of angels
Was alight, and its snow-packed ways
Sweet made (say the Evangels)
With the noise of their virelays.

Quem vidistis, pastores?
Why go ye feet unshod?
Wot ye within yon door is
Mary, the Mother of God?

No smoke of spice ascending
There—no roses are piled—
But, choicer than all balms blending,
There Mary hath kissed her Child.

MAY PROBYN

13. THE EPIPHANY

1.   As I ponder on the Epiphany, I pray once more for the grace to know our Lord more clearly, to be attracted by what I see, and to accept his values in my own life.

2.   It would be a mistake to interpret St Matthew's account (ch.2) as if he had written for us a literal narrative of the events. So we should not spend time now wondering how the star 'led' the Magi, how it halted over the stable, whether it was a comet or a nova or a conjunction of several planets. It would be equally mistaken to assume that none of the events took place, and that the story was pure legend with no basis of fact, invented for its symbolic value. The truth probably lies in between. The Gospel has taken an historical incident and elaborated it by applying to it various Old Testament passages, so as to use it as the vehicle for expressing the *meaning* of the events at the core of the story. The evangelist's meaning seems to be at least fourfold.

3.   (a) Jesus is the *fulfilment* of God's plans prophesied in the Old Testament. The priests and scribes quote Micah's prophecy that the coming king will be born in Bethlehem (2:6). The evangelist quotes on his own account three other prophecies: that the Lord's Son would be called from Egypt (2:15, quoting Hos 11:1); Jeremiah's prophecy concerning a massacre of children (2:18, quoting Jer 31:15); the prophecy that the Messiah would be called a Nazarene (2:23, quoting perhaps Is 11.1; 53:2, apparently taking 'Nazarene' to be derived from the Hebrew word for 'shoot'). From the very beginning everything in Jesus' life is the fulfilment of his Father's will, already foretold and initiated in the Old Testament.
  (b) Jesus is a *second Moses*. Jesus, like Moses, is saved from a massacre of baby boys (Ex 2:1–10; Mt 2:13); like Moses he has

to flee (Ex 2:15; Mt 2:14); like Moses he is called from Egypt (Ex 3:8; Mt 2:15); and it could be said of both Moses and Jesus that those who sought the child's life were dead (Ex 4:19; Mt 2:20). Later his temptations in the desert recapitulate those of the Israelites under Moses, and as Moses handed on to the people the Ten Commandments on Sinai, Jesus taught the principles of the New Commandment in an address on a mountain. Jesus is the legislator of the New Law, a law which deals with internal dispositions rather than mere external conformity, and is based on the fact that God is our Father.

(c) Jesus brings the good news to the *gentiles*, not only to Jews. (It is a sad theme of St Matthew's Gospel that the Jews reject their Messiah: 'the whole people' was to say to Pilate, 'His blood be on us and on our children': Mt 27:25). The Magi, who come to pay homage with their gifts, are presumably gentiles, and God sends a star to lead them, while the Jews ('Herod . . . and all Jerusalem with him': Mt 2:3) were 'troubled' by the report of the birth of a king of the Jews.

(d) Jesus is the *king* of the Jews (2:2, 6), foretold by Balaam under the sign of a star (Num 24:17). The Magi bring royal gifts (cf. Ps 72:10, 15; Is 60:6), and fall down in homage (v.11).

4.   We can learn from studying the different reactions of the people who come in contact with Jesus.

The Magi faithfully follow the star into the unknown. God does not give them all the guidance from the beginning: when the star disappears, they make inquiries; then God shows them the star again.

'I do not ask to see
The distant scene; one step enough for me.'
            (J. H. Newman, 'Lead kindly light')

When the star reappeared, 'they rejoiced exceedingly with great joy' (2:10). And when they found only a poor child, they still 'fell down and worshipped him. Then, opening their treasures, they

87

offered him gifts' (2:11). Finally they followed the sign God gave them to return by another way (2:12).

Herod, on the other hand, is 'troubled' by this threat to his position. He cunningly finds out from the Magi the age of the child (2:7), and has recourse to killing all the boys of the indicated age in order to get rid of this rival. Neither he nor the Jewish authorities seem able to entertain the possibility that they ought to welcome their king. Why not?

Joseph (like the patriarch Joseph, who was also guided by dreams) is urged by God's guidance from place to place, into the unknown with no warning. He had already been told in a dream not to be afraid to take Mary as his wife (1:20). Now he is told to take Mary and Jesus into Egypt (2:13); then after Herod's death back again to Israel (2:20), and finally into Galilee (2:22).

Mary is with the child when the Magi arrive; she possesses her son only to give him to others (2:11). Apart from that, her role in the narrative is purely passive: in a phrase that occurs four times Joseph is told to 'take the child and his mother' (2:13, 14, 20, 21).

Jesus is not only poor, but a refugee, not only utterly dependent on his mother and foster-father, but harried by political forces. In all this he is fulfilling his Father's will as expressed in the prophecies. He is not only the 'King of the Jews' and 'the Christ' or Messiah; he is the one whom all human beings should acknowledge. 'We have come to worship him' (2:2).

5.   We should not end without praying again for the grace to know, love and follow him.

Epiphany

Grace, thou source of each perfection,
   Favour from the height thy ray;
Thou the star of all direction,
   Child of endless truth and day.

Thou that bidst my cares be calmer,
   Lectur'd what to seek and shun,
Come, and guide a western palmer
   To the Virgin and her Son.

Lo! I travel in the spirit,
   On my knees my course I steer
To the house of might and merit
   With humility and fear.

. . .

From a heart serene and pleasant
   'Midst unnumber'd ills I feel,
I will meekly bring my present,
   And with sacred verses kneel.

. . .

Come, ye creatures of thanksgiving,
   Which are harmoniz'd to bless,
Birds that warble for your living,
   Beasts with ways of love express.

. . .

Ye that skill the flow'rs to fancy,
   And in just assemblage sort,
Pluck the primrose, pluck the pansy,
   And your prattling troop exhort:

'Little men, in Jesus mighty,
   And ye maids that go alone,
Bodies chaste, and spirits flighty,
   Ere the world and guilt are known,

'Breath so sweet, and cheeks so rosy—
   Put your little hands to pray,
Take ye ev'ry one a posy,
   And away to Christ, away.'—

Youth, benevolence, and beauty,
   In your Saviour's praise agree,
Which this day receives our duty,
   Sitting on the virgin's knee;

That from this day's institution
   Ev'ry penitent in deed,
At his hour of retribution
   As a child, through him may speed.

CHRISTOPHER SMART

INTERLUDE 2:
CRISIS IN PRAYER

In the earlier interlude on prayer I suggested a line of development that seems to be experienced by many people who give themselves seriously to prayer. (This is a subject on which one can generalize with some confidence, relying on a long tradition of spiritual writing in the Church, confirmed by one's own very limited experience acquired in attempting to advise others.) It may be well to repeat two points we have already seen; first, that the serious following of Christ needs the serious practice of prayer; secondly, that progress in prayer depends upon our desire for it. In the words of St Teresa of Avila, 'If we do not give ourselves to his Majesty as resolutely as he gives himself to us, he will be doing more than enough for us if he leaves us in mental prayer and from time to time visits us as he would visit servants in his vineyard. But these others are his beloved children, whom he would never want to banish from his side; and, as they have no desire to leave him, he never does so. He seats them at his table, and feeds them with his own food' (*Way of Perfection*, tr. Peers, ch.16). But be warned: if you really want to pray and try to pray, you may find yourself carried along paths you never dreamt of.

But, however much we desire to pray–or rather the more we desire to pray–progress in prayer is rarely smooth. Suddenly or gradually many people find themselves aparently unable to pray. When I find myself in that state, it is due either to a natural reason which is obstructing progress in prayer, or to a supernatural one which is a stage in my progress. It is important to consider which is true; not for the narcissistic pleasure of contemplating one's progress across the map of prayer, but simply because I may need to do something about it.

There can be many natural reasons: I may have stopped wanting to pray, and be merely going through the motions out of force of habit, or so that I may be able to credit myself with doing my duty; if so, I must try to rekindle my desire. I may have become so undisciplined in mind and heart that it is hard for me to still my seething brain; some formal procedures for calming the mind (deep breathing, upright kneeling, for example) may help, as well as some effective way of making sure that at least at the start and at the end I turn my gaze away from the fascinating kaleidoscope of life and fix it on the 'still point of the turning world,' perhaps by means of a scriptural text or image or thought that will focus it; but it may be that it is really the first difficulty over again, and I am not truly wanting to pray. It may be that I am tired and unwell, and that some physical remedy needs to be sought. It may be that I am resisting God's will.

This last cause of difficulty needs more attention. Prayer is not a reward for the perfect, but a lifeline for sinners, as the tax-gatherer in the parable knew. A sinner can come with his sin as well as his desire of God, can look Christ in the eye and confess his weakness, express his longing for healing, and beg for forgiveness; such a person can pray. A sinner can also come who is not yet strong enough to give up his sin; he too can confess his weakness and sincerely pray for healing, even before he has screwed up his will to reject the temptation: he too can pray. But the person who cannot pray is the one who cannot admit to himself or to God the fact that he is sinning; granted the desire to pray, the obstacle to prayer is not sin but the inability to acknowledge sin, for it implies that one is seeking security in self-approval rather than in God.

But it often happens that a person has the experience of being unable to pray, but cannot detect any of the natural causes suggested above. He wants to pray; he manages to calm and focus his attention; he is not particularly tired or unwell; he is not aware of any tendency to hide from God's will. He may find that when he is not formally praying thoughts about God come easily, and even that in odd moments of the day his mind gravitates readily to God. But yet when he tries to give himself up to prayer, it seems impossible to pray. This impossibility might take the form of a persistent turmoil of distractions; or a dry emptiness; or even the feeling of being enveloped in a mental fog. The important thing to realize is that this experience may not be a failure in prayer, the inability to accept the form of prayer which God is trying to give me, but a stage in the progress of my prayer which is according to God's plan.

This can be true in two ways. First, it often seems to happen that God wishes to make prayer difficult, in order to purify our faith. When prayer is easy and consoling, we may be praying for the sake of the pleasant experience. Or we may pray so as to be able to give ourselves the credit for praying. God is not content with this; when we are strong enough he takes away the sweetness so that the only consideration that can sustain us in prayer is the desire for God himself. We have to trust his promise that if we seek him we find him, even though he seems to remain hidden. For this reason such prayer in the dark is sometimes called the prayer of faith.

The second explanation is rather different, though it may be true at the same time as the first. This state of spiritual darkness is seen not so much as an inability to pray, but as a state of prayer, however hard it may be at first to recognize. Prayer, we have seen, is the raising of the mind and heart to God, especially the heart. This movement of the heart to God is usually clad, at least in our early experiences, in some recognizable form of words or gestures: we say prayers, we genuflect. But the words or the gestures are the cladding and not the thing itself. What is happening in this obscure prayer is that the movement of the heart is there with little recognizable expression. A medieval English mystic called it the 'naked intent unto God.'

People can be in this state for a long time without recognizing it. When it is put to them for the first time that what they are experiencing may not be the inability to pray but this hidden prayer, almost invariably their reaction seems to be: 'This can't be true in my case; I'm not holy enough.'

It is important to try to recognize this state, not of course in order to be able to congratulate ourselves on our progress–for it is God's doing; but because if we fail to recognize it we may react in a way that is very harmful to ourselves. The worst reaction is simply to conclude that we can't pray, and that it's no use trying; so we don't seriously give the time to prayer at all, filling the time with soothing little chores like shaving or cleaning our teeth; or we do something we think more useful, like reading the Bible or a spiritual book. Of course, reading can be prayer; but the depth of prayer involved in reading is often much shallower than that which is involved in standing face to face with God, with no words coming between us.

How then can we recognize this state? Let us assume the natural explanations given above do not seem an adequate explanation; that we sincerely want to pray and are entering prayer with a still and focused mind. There are two ways of detecting it. The first sign is the existence of a contrast between the ready interest with which we contact God in moments when we are not formally praying and the blanket of fog or the utter dryness we experience in our times of explicit prayer. The second is the test our Lord himself proposed: by their fruits you shall know them (cf. Mt 7:16). If we can honestly say that we are trying (though never perfectly) to live an unselfish and faithful Christian life, the Holy Spirit must be in our prayer. One further test should be applied if we are wise, namely to discuss the matter with a spiritual director, if possible one who knows us.

If after careful thought it seems that the prayer we are experiencing is this obscure prayer, which St John of the Cross called the Dark Night and the medieval English mystic already quoted called the Cloud of Unknowing, what have we to do? Clearly we must go on trying to pray; but what we must not do is to try to force this naked intent unto God into some recognizable clothes; generally we shall not be able to do it, anyhow, however hard we try. All we can do is to begin with a still mind and with a very brief prayer for the grace to pray. It may help to have a thought or a phrase from scripture with which to begin. After that, all we may be able to do is to try to hold ourselves peacefully before God in our darkness. Distractions often teem, because if the imagination finds nothing to grasp in the prayer itself the vacuum tends to be filled with irrelevancies. When we recognize distractions, we gently put them aside. But they scarcely matter, because our hearts are directed lovingly towards God. Sometimes we may become aware of this attention to God. We may sometimes be able to recognize it at the moment of switching it off when we come to the end of our formal prayer.

This prayer can be tiring. Occasionally to repeat a text may help to break any tension. But in this kind of prayer methods of praying are irrelevant. The only thing we need to do is to try not to get in the way of the working of the Holy Spirit. The advice may be open to abuse, but one spiritual writer wrote that entering into a period of prayer of this kind is rather like composing oneself for sleep.

Finally, it is possible that the type of prayer God wants to give us will vary according to our needs. There may be times when, instead of the prayer of darkness, what I need is a more thoughtful prayer in which I think through a problem in God's presence; or a prayer of petition, when I ask for help for myself or another. We can only pray as God gives us to pray; but we need regularly to examine our prayer to see if we have become insensitive to the leading of the Holy Spirit.

14. THE MIND OF CHRIST

1. As usual, we pray for the grace to know Christ more clearly, love him more dearly and follow him more nearly. In this meditation we consider some of the glimpses the gospels give us of his mind.

2. It is appropriate at this point in the retreat to begin looking at our daily lives and our future, and to ask ourselves what changes we need to make. The introduction contains some paragraphs which discuss the various sorts of decision with which a retreatant may be faced (pp.15–17). In order to be sure that we are taking our decisions for the right reasons, we need to be familiar with Jesus' way of thinking and to try and share it.

3. 'And when it was day he departed [from Capernaum] and went into a lonely place. And the people sought him and came to him, and would have kept him from leaving them; but he said to them, "I must preach the good news of the kingdom of God to other cities also; for I was sent for this purpose"' (Lk 4:42–3).

4. At Nain he comes upon the funeral of the only son of a widow. 'And when the Lord saw her, he had compassion on her and said to her, "Do not weep." And he came and touched the bier, and the bearers stood still. And he said, "Young man, I say to you, arise." And the dead man sat up, and began to speak. And he gave him to his mother' (Lk 7:13–15).

5. 'Take my yoke upon you, and learn from me; for I am gentle and lowly in heart, and you will find rest for your souls. For my yoke is easy, and my burden is light' (Mt 11.29–30).

6.   (After Peter has professed his faith that Jesus is the Christ, the Son of the living God) 'From that time Jesus began to show his disciples that he must go to Jerusalem and suffer many things from the elders and chief priests and scribes, and be killed, and on the third day be raised. And Peter took him and began to rebuke him, saying, "God forbid, Lord! This shall never happen to you." But he turned and said to Peter, "Get behind me, Satan! You are a hindrance to me; for you are not on the side of God, but of men"' (Mt 16:21–3).

7.   (When the disciples offer him food) 'Jesus said to them, "My food is to do the will of him who sent me, and to accomplish his work. Do you not say, There are yet four months, then comes the harvest? I tell you, lift up your eyes, and see how the fields are already white for the harvest"' (Jn 4:34–5).

8.   'We must work the works of him who sent me, while it is day; night comes, when no one can work' (Jn 9:4). 'I came to cast fire upon the earth; and would that it were already kindled! I have a baptism to be baptized with; and how I am constrained until it is accomplished!' (Lk 12:49–50). 'Then he went home; and the crowd came together again, so that they could not even eat. And when his family heard it, they went out to seize him, for people said, "He is beside himself"' (Mk 3:19–21).

9.   (When they are caught by a storm in a boat) 'He was in the stern, asleep on the cushion; and they woke him and said to him, "Teacher, do you not care if we perish?" And he awoke and rebuked the wind, and said to the sea, "Peace! Be still!" And the wind ceased, and there was a great calm. He said to them, "Why are you afraid? Have you no faith?" And they were filled with awe and said to one another, "Who then is this, that even wind and sea obey him?"' (Mk 4:38–41).

10.   'Have this mind among yourselves which is yours in Christ

D

Jesus, who, though he was in the form of God, did not count equality with God a thing to be grasped, but emptied himself, taking the form of a servant, being born in the likeness of men. And being found in human form he humbled himself and became obedient unto death, even death on a cross. Therefore God has highly exalted him . . .' (Phil 2:5–9).

From the Spiritual Exercises of St Ignatius:

INTRODUCTION TO DECISION-MAKING

In order to make right decisions, for our part, the eye of our intention needs to be simple, so that I concentrate my attention on the reason why I was created, namely for the praise of our Lord God and the salvation of my soul. Accordingly I should choose only those things which help me to attain the end for which I was created, for the means should be subordinated and directed to the end and not vice versa. But many, for example, first choose to marry, which is a means, and secondly to serve our Lord God in the married state, though the service of God should be the end. Similarly there are others who first seek to hold ecclesiastical benefices, and afterwards to serve God in them. Such people do not move straight towards God, but want God to come straight to their own disordered desires. Thus they make the end into a means and the means into an end, taking last what they ought to take first (n.169).

We should only make a decision about things which are either indifferent or good in themselves, and are of service to our holy mother the hierarchical Church, and are not evil or opposed to the Church (n.170).

Some matters call for an irrevocable decision, e.g. to seek ordination or to get married. About other matters a decision can be changed, for example, the acceptance or renunciation of benefices or secular goods (n.171).

If we have made an irrevocable decision, say, about marriage, ordination, etc., no further choice remains open to us in the matter, because our decision cannot be reversed. But it should be observed that if someone has made such a choice without the due order [of means and ends] and under the influence of irregular attachments, all he can do is to repent of his fault, and take care to lead a good life in the state he has chosen (n.172).

But if, concerning a matter which can be changed, we have taken a decision which was not sincerely made from the right motives, and desire to achieve something which is worthwhile and pleasing to God, it will be helpful to subject the matter to a fresh decision in the proper way (n.174).

N.B. Those who are committed to a state of matrimony or ecclesiastical office, whether they possess much property or not, may have no opportunity or strong desire to make a decision about matters which can be changed. In that case it will be helpful if, instead of going through a formal process of decision-making, they are shown some method of amending and reforming their personal life and the performance of their duties.

They should recall that they were created and given their state in life for the glory and praise of our Lord God and the salvation of their souls. To achieve this end, they should reflect deeply, with the help of the methods given for decision-making,[1] how large a house they ought to keep, and how many servants; what their relations with their servants should be; how they should instruct them by word and example. So too with regard to their income: how much they should apply to household expenses, and how much should be given to the poor and other charities. They should desire and seek nothing else save that our Lord God should be praised and glorified in everything. For everyone should keep it in mind that their progress in

---

1 St Ignatius gives two methods of reaching a decision: the first consists of the prayerful weighing of the pros and cons (nn.178–183); the second involves viewing the matter with detachment, considering what advice to offer someone else in a similar situation, or asking ourselves which course we would wish we had taken on our deathbed (nn.184–188).

any spiritual matter is proportionate to their renunciation of self-love, self-seeking and self-interest (n.189).

The Call

Come, my Way, my Truth, my Life!
Such a Way as gives us breath,
Such a Truth as ends all strife,
Such a Life as killeth Death.

Come, my Light, my Feast, my Strength!
Such a Light as shows a feast,
Such a Feast as mends in length,
Such a Strength as makes his guest.

Come, my Joy, my Love, my Heart!
Such a Joy as none can move,
Such a Love as none can part,
Such a Heart as joys in love.

GEORGE HERBERT

15. TRUE AND FALSE VALUES

1. In this meditation the grace we ask for is that we may understand our Lord's temptations and join him in rejecting them; and that we may understand and be attracted by the values according to which he lived and which he commended to his followers in the form of the Beatitudes. It is not a question of intellectual understanding, but of feeling Christ's principles in our bones. This then is another form of our customary prayer that we may know him, love him and follow him. We pray too that any decision we have to make during the retreat may be made according to these principles of our Lord.

2. We should not bother to ask ourselves here how exactly our Lord experienced these temptations, or how the Evangelists learned of them. What we have in the fourth chapters of Matthew and Luke is an account of these temptations written in a highly symbolic way; whether this explanation is our Lord's own, or that of the Evangelists, does not matter here. Our Lord's forty days in the desert corresponds with the Israelites' forty years, and with Moses' fast of forty days and forty nights, when he neither ate bread nor drank water (Ex 34:28; cf. Lk 4:2). 'You shall remember all the way which the Lord your God has led you these forty years in the wilderness, that he might humble you, testing you to know what was in your heart, whether you would keep his commandments, or not' (Deut 8:2). Each temptation is the mirror-image of one of the Israelites' temptations; and in each case the reply with which our Lord rebuffs the devil is taken from Deuteronomy, where the Israelites are rebuked for falling into sin. We might see the temptations as the process by which our Lord wrestled to discover his Father's will, to discover what sort of Messiah his Father wished him to be. Or we might see the devil trying to discover whether Jesus really was the Son of God

by putting before him less perfect ideas of the Messiahship. We need to remember that there were current at the time many different understandings of what the Messiah would be. Jesus rejects the notion of a Messiah who will win an easy following by a show of miracles and instead chooses to be the humble Messiah of Zechariah 9:9, or the suffering servant of Isaiah 53.

3.   The first temptation, to turn the stones into bread, corresponds to the temptation of the Israelites who grumbled against God and forced him to work a miracle so as to provide them with manna in the desert (Ex 16:2–18); there was a tradition that the Messiah would be a miracle-working conjurer (cf. Lk 23:8). Jesus in reply borrows words from Deuteronomy 8:3 to the effect that God gave the Israelites manna in order to teach them that man does not live on bread alone.

4.   The Israelites had also lost faith and grumbled against God when they were thirsty, and forced God to provide them with water from the rock (Num 20:2–13). Jesus in a second temptation is invited to force God to work the miracle of preventing him from hurting himself if he jumps down from the pinnacle of the temple. The devil quotes Psalm 91, to the effect that God will protect those whom he loves by sending his angels to catch them so that they do not trip over a stone. Jesus replies by quoting words from Deuteronomy 6:16: 'You shall not put the Lord to the test,' meaning that it was wrong for the Israelites to force God's hand. In applying the words to his own situation Jesus means not that it is wrong for the devil to tempt him, though of course it is, but that it would be wrong if he, Jesus, forced his Father's hand.

5.   The Israelites in the desert worshipped the golden calf (Ex 32:1–8). The devil tempts Jesus to worship him. This seems a very crass temptation, but perhaps the point is that Jesus is offered a compromise: the devil will give him a following if he

will acknowledge the devil's rights. Jesus replies in words taken from Deuteronomy 6:13–14, forbidding the Israelites to worship false gods.

6. If we consider our own temptations at this stage in the retreat, we might envisage not so much temptations to sin as temptations to accept a lower standard, a compromise between what God wants and what we are inclined towards. We must pray that in any decisions we have to take we may seek solely God's will.

7. Let us now look at the values which our Lord recommended to his followers. They are set out in the Beatitudes (Mt 5:3–12), which Jesus delivered on the mountain, the second Moses delivering the New Law. They take the form of a series of statements. 'Blessed are . . .' Some translations use the word 'Happy' instead of 'Blessed'. 'Happy' is not a well-chosen word, because it suggests pleasure or enjoyment, which is not our Lord's point. 'Blessed' sounds too churchy. What our Lord means is that we are fortunate, enjoying a good thing, living in the right sort of way, on the right lines, if our lives show the qualities spoken of in the Beatitudes.

8. What sort of people does our Lord regard as living on the right lines? The poor in spirit, the mourners, the meek, those who hunger and thirst for righteousness, the merciful, the pure in heart, the peacemakers, those who are persecuted for the sake of justice, and those who are reviled and spoken evil of. St Luke's version is even more austere. The fortunate ones are simply the poor, not the poor in spirit; the hungry, not those who hunger after justice; those who weep. In case we should miss his point, St Luke gives us a matching set of condemnations of those who have the opposite qualities: 'Woe to you that are rich . . .', 'Woe to you that are full . . .', 'Woe to you that laugh . . .', 'Woe to you when all men speak well of you . . .' (6:20–6).

9. These are hard words. There is obviously a temptation to water them down. Perhaps all that we can say is that in making our choices we must show at least a willingness to accept poverty, unpopularity, etc., if it should come our way. If on the other hand we make our choices simply in order to avoid poverty, unpopularity and the other signs of a life which is fortunate in God's eyes, our choice is likely to be a bad one.

10. Our Lord himself lived by his Beatitudes. We should pray that we may make his principles of life our own. This is a grace: we cannot achieve it by our own willpower. We may find that in making this meditation the thought of following the Beatitudes in their starkness repels or frightens us. We may not understand our Lord's mind, but since this is what he asks of us, we accept it and want it, because we want him.

From the Spiritual Exercises of St Ignatius:

THE TWO STANDARDS

The first standard is that of Christ our supreme Leader and Lord, the second that of Lucifer, the deadly enemy of the human race.

The preparatory prayer takes the usual form (n.136).

The first prelude is a consideration of the facts, how Christ and Lucifer each summon human beings to rally round their standards (n.137).

The second prelude is the composition of place. We should imagine a vast plain covering the whole region of Jerusalem where Christ our Lord, the supreme Leader of the good, has taken his station; and another plain in the region of Babylon where the leader of our enemies Lucifer stands (n.138).

The third prelude is to ask for what I desire. Here it is to pray for knowledge of the deceits of the evil leader and for strength to guard against them; and for knowledge of the true way of life shown by our supreme and true Leader and for grace to imitate him (n.139).

The first point is to imagine the leader of all our enemies in the great plain of Babylon seated on a great throne of fire and smoke, a hideous and terrifying sight (n.140).

The second point is to observe how he calls together countless demons and dispatches them all over the world to this city or that, omitting no province, place, state or individual (n.141).

The third point is to notice the instructions he gives them, urging them to snare human beings in nets and chains, leading them, in most cases, first to the desire of wealth, so that they may more easily be led to the quest for worldly honours, and finally to overweening pride. Thus the first step consists of wealth, the second of honours, and the third of pride; and from these three steps he leads them on to all the other vices (n.142).

By contrast we should consider Christ, our supreme and true Leader and Lord, under the same heads (n.143).

The first point is to observe Christ standing in a simple place on a great plain in the region near Jerusalem, attractive and lovable in appearance, (n.144).

The second point is to see how the Lord of the universe chooses so many people, apostles, disciples, etc., and sends them out all over the world to spread his sacred doctrine of salvation among human beings of every class and condition (n.145).

The third point is to hear the message which Christ our Lord delivers to his servants and friends whom he is sending out on this task. He instructs them to seek to help the whole human race: first they are to lead others to the highest spiritual poverty, and even material poverty, if it is the will of the

Divine Majesty to choose them for it; then they are to draw others on to the desire for ridicule and contempt; for from these two things humility grows. Thus there are three steps: first, poverty as opposed to wealth, ridicule or mockery as opposed to worldly honours, and humility as opposed to pride; and these three steps lead to all the other virtues (n.146).

After that I should address a colloquy to our Lady, asking her to obtain for me from her Son and Lord the favour of being admitted under his standard: first in the highest spiritual poverty or even in material poverty if it pleases the Divine Majesty to choose me and admit me to such a state; secondly in ridicule and insults, so that I may imitate him more closely, provided that I can suffer these things without sin on anyone's part or offence against the Divine Majesty. I shall conclude this first colloquy with the Hail Mary.[1]

I then ask the Son to obtain the same favour for me from the Father, and then say the Anima Christi.

I then ask the Father to grant this request, and say the Our Father (n.147).

Avarice

Money, thou bane of bliss and source of woe,
    Whence com'st thou, that thou art so fresh and fine?
    I know thy parentage is base and low—
Man found thee poor and dirty in a mine.

Surely thou didst so little contribute,
    To this great kingdom which thou now hast got,
    That he was fain, when thou wast destitute,
To dig thee out of thy dark cave and grot.

1 For this prayer and the others mentioned in the colloquies, see Appendix.

Then forcing thee, by fire he made thee bright:
  Nay, thou hast got the face of man; for we
  Have with our stamp and seal transferred our right;
Thou art the man, and man but dross to thee!

Man calleth thee his wealth, who made thee rich;
And while he digs out thee, falls in the ditch.

GEORGE HERBERT

God be in my head,
And in my understanding;
God be in mine eyes,
And in my looking;
God be in my mouth,
And in my speaking;
God be in my heart,
And in my thinking;
God be at my end and at my departing.

ANON.

16. HONESTY BEFORE GOD

1. I should see myself before God, seeking his will. This is especially true if I have a decision to make. His will which I seek is not a stern command, but what is most in accordance with his goodness. The grace that I seek is that I may choose what is for his greater glory and my own greater good in any decision I have to make during the retreat and in all the little decisions in my daily life, and that I may gain a deeper insight into the *psychology of self-deception*, so that this insight may form the pattern of my thinking every time I am faced with a choice. We are thinking at this stage of the right frame of mind for making a decision *before* God's will is discovered, rather than our attitude to his will once it is discovered. The grace that I seek, then, is honesty with God and myself.

2. There are three possible attitudes: (a) *spiritual paralysis* (known to the medievals as *accidie*), when we see the need to make some decision, but cannot bring ourselves to make it, allowing ourselves instead to drift along as before; (b) *tokenism*, when we see the need to take action of some sort, but appease our conscience by making a token choice about a side-issue, without facing the need to make a choice about the substantive point; (c) *spiritual honesty*. Indeed, in a serious matter, I may want to be so certain that I shall not be a victim of self-deception that, if I am strongly inclined to one possible course of action rather than the other, I represent to myself as a real possibility that God's will may be the opposite of what I would like to choose, and may even pray for the opposite of what I naturally prefer. For example, I may be living in a country with an unjust regime and wondering whether I should leave it; my inclinations may be all in favour of staying. If I am guilty of *accidie*, I will say to myself, 'Yes, perhaps I ought to think about leaving,' but

never do anything about it. If I try to appease my conscience with a token, instead of deciding whether I ought to leave, I may decide how much money I should give to help the families of political prisoners. If my dispositions are right I might pray: 'Lord, I would love to stay so much that I'm afraid I'm not fit to find out what *you* want. But I admit it as a serious possibility that you may want me to go. The safest thing is for me to pray that that *may* be what you want. If it is not so, please make it clear to me.'

3.   The Rich Young Man was faced with the choice whether to follow Jesus or not (Mt 19:16–22). He is seeking the good: 'What good deed must I do, to have eternal life?' He is an upright man: he has kept all the commandments. He feels himself drawn to some undefined higher ideal: 'What do I still lack?' (19:20). St Mark depicts him even more attractively: he 'ran up and knelt before' Jesus (10:17); 'and Jesus looking upon him loved him' (10:21). The answer held out to him is more than he can bring himself to take: 'If you would be perfect ['you lack one thing' (Mk 10:21)], go, sell what you possess and give to the poor, and you will have treasure in heaven; and come, follow me' (Mt 19:21). Jesus is trying to shake him out of his tokenism, and bring him to give nothing less than his whole self. 'At that saying his countenance fell, and he went away sorrowful; for he had great possessions. And Jesus looked around and said to his disciples, "How hard it will be for those who have riches to enter the kingdom of God!"' (Mk 10:22–3).

4.   We can see other examples of men who are willing to give anything less than what they want to keep, in Lk 9:57–62. 'Whoever of you does not renounce all that he has cannot be my disciple' (Lk 14:33). We cannot by will-power bring ourselves to this pitch of generosity. Very likely all that we can do in this meditation is to pray for the grace to leave everything and follow Jesus (cf. Mk 10:28).

From the Spiritual Exercises of St Ignatius:

THREE CLASSES OF MEN.

A meditation to help us to choose what we see to be the better alternative.

The preparatory prayer is as usual (n.149).

For the first prelude, the review of the facts, I should consider three different classes of person. Each has acquired £10,000 without reference to the glory and love of God, but they now wish to save their souls and be at peace with our Lord God by freeing themselves of the weight of their attachment to this property (n.150).

The second prelude, in which I imagine a place, consists of setting myself in the presence of our Lord God and all his saints, so that I may know and desire what is more pleasing to his divine Goodness (n.151).

The third prelude is to ask for what I desire, namely the grace to choose what is more conducive to the glory of his divine Majesty and the salvation of my soul (n.152).

A person of the first class does wish to be rid of the attraction of his property so as to be at peace with our Lord God and save his soul, but as long as he lives he never takes the necessary steps (n.153).

A person of the second class also desires to be rid of the attachment, but in such a way as to remain in possession of the property in question, so as to make God come to his own way of thinking. He is not resolved to give the property up in order to go to God, even if that is the better way for him (n.154).

A person of third class also wishes to be free from the attachment, but in such a way as not to be influenced by any desire either to retain the property or not to retain it. He wishes to desire or not to desire the property only to the extent that our Lord God directs his will, and according to what he judges to be most conducive to the service and praise of his divine Majesty.

Meanwhile he seeks to act as if he had already given it all up in his heart, endeavouring not to desire that thing or anything else, unless he is moved to do so solely by the service of our Lord God, so that it is the desire of being better able to serve our Lord God which moves him to take the thing or to leave it (n.155).

The same three colloquies are made as in the previous meditation on the Two Standards[1] (n.156).

N.B. When we experience an attraction or repugnance contrary to material poverty, and we are not equally inclined towards poverty or wealth, in order to put an end to the disordered attraction it is very useful to ask in the colloquies, even if nature rebels, that the Lord will choose us to live in material poverty, and to affirm that we desire, pray and beg for it, provided only that it is to the service and praise of his divine Goodness (n.157).

(During his Courtship)

Christ, my Life, my Only Treasure,
    Thou alone
    Mould thine own,
After thy Good pleasure.

Thou, who paidst my Price, direct me!
    Thine I am,
    Holy Lamb,
Save, and always save me.

Order Thou my whole Condition,
    Chuse my State,
    Fix my Fate
By thy wise Decision.

1 See p.106.

From all Earthly Expectation
    Set me free,
    Seize for Thee
  All my Strength of Passion.

Into absolute Subjection
    Be it brought,
    Every Thought,
  Every fond Affection.

That which most my Soul requires
    For thy sake
    Hold it back
  Purge my Best Desires.

Keep from me thy lovliest Creature,
    Till I prove
    JESUS' Love
  Infinitely sweeter;

Till with purest Passion panting
    Cries my Heart
    'Where Thou art
  Nothing more is wanting.'

Blest with thine Abiding Spirit,
    Fully blest
    Now I rest,
  All in Thee inherit.

Heaven is now with Jesus given;
    Christ in me,
    Thou shalt be
  Mine Eternal Heaven.

CHARLES WESLEY

17. THE PASCHAL SHAPE
OF LIFE

1. By the end of this section of the retreat we should have made any decisions that we had set ourselves to make, even if the decision may have to be of an interim nature: 'I haven't yet been able to reach clarity over this matter; therefore for the time being I will do X, while taking steps Y and Z which will help me to reach a final decision.' This meditation therefore is the last that we make in our search to assimilate Christ's values, so that we may make our decision according to those values.

2. In St John's account of Palm Sunday, some Greeks ask Philip (who has himself a Greek name) to take them to Jesus. Jesus' reaction is to make an uncompromising statement of his principles: 'The hour has come for the Son of man to be glorified. Truly, truly, I say to you, unless a grain of wheat falls into the earth and dies, it remains alone; but if it dies, it bears much fruit. He who loves his life loses it, and he who hates his life in this world will keep it for eternal life' (Jn 12:23–5). In other words, all spiritual achievement comes through a spiritual death. This is the Paschal shape of life, a death-resurrection pattern. In the following of Christ, as well as in business, there is no such thing as a free lunch.

3. Jesus himself was about to experience this in his own life. His death was not to be the end; it was followed by the resurrection. The most natural way of expressing this is to say that his death was followed by his glory. This is not St John's way of speaking, however: the cross itself is already the glory; 'the hour' in which he is to be glorified is the hour of Calvary (Jn 12:23). It is when Judas has gone out to betray him that Jesus

says, 'Now is the Son of man glorified' (Jn 13:31). Jesus' glory is
the visible manifestation of his godhead. It is in self-sacrifice that
the godhead is most revealed, because 'God is love' (1 Jn 4:16).

4.   We considered in section 14 how, when Jesus predicted his
passion, Peter, with his natural affection for Jesus, unwittingly
played the part of Satan and tried to dissuade his Master. In the
next episode in St Mark we see Jesus making it clear to his
disciples that they too will have to go through suffering: 'If any
man would come after me, let him deny himself and take up his
cross and follow me. For whoever would save his life will lose it;
and whoever loses his life for my sake and the gospel's will save
it' (Mk 8:34–35).

5.   Why did Christ have to suffer? To save us–yes, but why this
way? We shall have more to say about this in Part Four. For the
time being we can say: (a) Jesus sees the passion as his Father's
will: to lay down his life is the 'charge I have received from my
Father' (Jn 10:18); he 'became obedient unto death, even death
on a cross' (Phil 2:8); (b) Jesus sees self-sacrifice as a death to
self and a source of spiritual fruitfulness; his own self-sacrifice
involves a literal death.

6.   Consequently we should pray for the grace to put on Christ's
mind, not taking a masochistic pleasure in self-sacrifice, but
trusting in Jesus' assurance about the positive power of self-
sacrifice. But self-sacrifice will only be a source of power if it is
loving, not morbid.

7.   But there is a further grace we can pray for: the grace to
desire to experience the cross simply for the sake of being like
Jesus. 'Far be it from me to glory except in the cross of our Lord
Jesus Christ, by which the world has been crucified to me, and I
to the world' (Gal 6:14). 'For the word of the cross is folly to
those who are perishing, but to us who are being saved it is the

power of God . . . For the foolishness of God is wiser than men, and the weakness of God is stronger than men' (1 Cor 1:18, 25). 'As we share abundantly in Christ's sufferings, so through Christ we share abundantly in comfort too' (2 Cor 1:5).

8.   This desire to share in Christ's sufferings is not something that can be readily justified by logic. Someone deeply in love may wish to share the sufferings of the loved one, but we do not regard it as right for someone in pain to want other people to share his suffering. Yet this desire to share Christ's cross is not only urged by the words of St Paul we have just considered, and a characteristic of the saints; it is supported by Christ's own words in the gospels: 'If any man would come after me, let him deny himself and take up his cross and follow me' (Mk 8:34). St Ignatius Loyola calls this desire to suffer with Jesus 'the third degree of humility'. Karl Rahner describes it as follows: 'a love for the cross of the Lord is lived out that no longer seeks this-worldly reasons. It is simply presupposed that whoever follows the Lord and Master, the Crucified, him who is a scandal and foolishness to the world, is on the right path' (*Spiritual Exercises*, p.199).

9.   This desire to be one with Christ in his suffering can exist at various levels. At its lowest, we can *accept* suffering from God's hand because it unites us with Christ. At the next level, we can *welcome* it for the same reason. The saints, however, have attained to a higher level, and have been given the grace positively to desire the cross. In making this meditation we may well find the prospect of the cross frightening and repulsive. Even so, our prayer will be very good if we can honestly admit our cowardice and sincerely ask that, in spite of it, we may be able to carry a little cross in the Lord's footsteps, simply because we have his word that there is no other way of being with him.

10.   This frame of mind, at least the desire of the desire of the

cross, is the necessary condition for making a Christian choice. This does not mean that the hardest thing is necessarily the right thing to choose; if I am trying to decide how best to serve other people, I must seek what is for their good, not the spiritual luxury of what is toughest for myself; I have no right to choose a cross for other people. But unless we value the cross, our choices are likely to be influenced by consideration of our own comfort or credit or power.

11. So the keynote of this meditation will be *prayer* for this grace which we cannot possibly attain by our own resources: love of the cross for love of the crucified.

From the Spiritual Exercises of St Ignatius:

THREE KINDS OF HUMILITY

The first kind of humility is that which is necessary for eternal salvation. In it I abase and humble myself as far as possible so as in all things to obey the law of our Lord God, so that, even to gain power over the whole world or to save my life, I would not consider transgressing any divine or human command which binds under pain of mortal sin (n.165).

The second kind involves a higher state of perfection. It consists of a disposition not to desire or value wealth rather than poverty, reputation rather than ill-repute, a long life rather than a short one, provided each alternative is equally conducive to the service of our Lord God and the salvation of my soul. At the same time, I would not, for the whole world or to save my life, consider committing a venial sin (n.166).

The third is the most perfect kind of humility, and presupposes the first two. In this kind, even if God's praise and glory are equally served on both sides, for the sake of imitating Christ our Lord and being more like him, I desire and choose poverty with the poor Christ rather than wealth, insults with the insulted Christ rather than honours; and I desire to be regarded as a useless fool for the sake of Christ, who was so regarded before me, rather than wise and prudent in this world (n.167).

To attain this third kind of humility it will be very helpful to make the three colloquies described above in the meditation on the Three Classes,[1] begging that our Lord will be pleased to choose us for this third kind of humility, which is greater and better, in order the better to imitate and serve him, provided the equal or greater service and praise of his divine Majesty is involved (n.168).

Crucifixion to the World by the Cross of Christ

(Galatians 6:14)
When I survey the wondrous Cross
Where the young Prince of Glory died,
My richest gain I count but loss,
And pour contempt on all my pride.

Forbid it, Lord, that I should boast
Save in the death of Christ, my God;
All the vain things that charm me most,
I sacrifice them to his blood.

See from his head, his hands, his feet,
Sorrow and love flow mingled down;
Did e'er such love and sorrow meet?
Or thorns compose so rich a crown?

His dying crimson like a robe
Spreads o'er his body on the Tree,
Then am I dead to all the globe,
And all the globe is dead to me.

1. See pp.106 and 111.

Were the whole realm of nature mine,
That were a present far too small;
Love so amazing, so divine,
Demands my soul, my life, my all.

ISAAC WATTS

PART THREE: THE PASSION OF OUR LORD

18. THE LAST SUPPER

1. St John prefaces his account of the Last Supper with these words: 'Now before the feast of the Passover, when Jesus knew that his hour had come to *depart* out of this world to the Father, having loved his own who were in the world, he loved them to the end' (Jn 13:1). St Luke tells us that at the Transfiguration Moses and Elijah appeared and spoke to Jesus 'of the *departure*, which he was to accomplish at Jerusalem' (Lk 9:31). The Greek word for 'departure' is *exodus*, the traditional term used to describe the rescue of the Israelites from their slavery in Egypt, and their journey to the Promised Land. St John reminds us that Jesus' exodus was at the Passover, the feast of the Jewish exodus. Jesus' own exodus, achieved at the cost of his death and resurrection, makes our exodus possible.

2. St John's words are not only of great solemnity: they speak of Jesus' utter love for his people. 'He loved them to the end'–to the end of his life, to the utmost limit of love. St Luke introduces the Last Supper with a similar thought on our Lord's own lips: 'I have earnestly desired to eat this passover with you before I suffer' (Lk 22:15). Knox's translation is more eloquent: 'I have longed and longed to share this meal with you'; so too is his translation of Jn 13:1: 'He still loved those who were his own, whom he was leaving in the world, and he would give them the uttermost proof of his love.' The grace that we ask for in this meditation is to understand something of this longing and this love of Jesus.

3. In all the Gospel accounts of the Last Supper there is a sense of the sadness of parting. In St John there is in addition a feeling

of urgency: 'I have yet many things to say to you, but you cannot bear them now' (Jn 16:12). So into this last meal with his disciples Jesus compresses a fourfold last testament: he leaves them a symbol, a command, a promise and a gift.

4. A symbol: he takes a bowl of water, puts on an apron and performs the humble service (welcome to people walking without socks in a hot and dusty climate) of washing his disciples' feet. The purpose is to give them an acted lesson that would be engraved in their memories after he had left them: 'If I then, your Lord and Teacher, have washed your feet, you also ought to wash one another's feet' (Jn 13:14).

5. A command: 'A new commandment I give to you that you love one another' (Jn 13:34). In the other Gospels, Jesus has already given this new commandment: 'You shall love the Lord your God with all your heart, and with all your soul, and with all your mind. This is the great and first commandment. And the second is like it, You shall love your neighbour as yourself. On these two commandments depend all the law and the prophets' (Mt 22:37–40). The command to love is therefore the fundamental Christian commandment: 'By this all men will know that you are my disciples, if you have love for one another' (Jn 13:35). It is to be a love without limits. 'This is my commandment, that you love one another as I have loved you. Greater love has no man than this, that a man lay down his life for his friend' (Jn 15:12–13).

6. A promise: Jesus has to go, but 'I will not leave you desolate. I will come to you ... The Counsellor [Paraclete], the Holy Spirit, whom the Father will send in my name, he will teach you all things, and bring to your remembrance all that I have said to you ... It is to your advantage that I go away, for if I do not go away, the Counsellor will not come to you; but if I go, I will send

him to you' (Jn 14:18, 26; 16:7). Our Lord's meaning seems to be that it is by the Holy Spirit that he will remain with his Church.

7. A gift: the gift of himself which is the Holy Eucharist. 'He took bread, and blessed, and broke it, and gave it to them, and said, "Take; this is my body." And he took a cup . . . and he said to them, "This is my blood of the covenant, which is poured out for many"' (Mk 14:22-4). Moses had inaugurated the old covenant with the blood of slaughtered animals: 'Behold the blood of the covenant which the Lord has made with you' (Ex 24:8); Jesus inaugurates the new covenant for his new people in his own blood. The actions with the bread and wine denote his own life which is sacrificed for the forgiveness of our sins; without this prophetic action, would the apostles have understood the significance of his death? It is a sacrifice with which Christ's followers are themselves caught up as they celebrate it with thanksgiving. It is the gift of himself to be the 'Bread of Life' (Jn 6:35). For his own reasons St John does not recount the institution of the Eucharist in his narrative of the Last Supper; instead he gives earlier a long sermon of Jesus on the Eucharist, in which the words at the Supper are anticipated: 'the bread which I shall give for the life of the world is my flesh' (Jn 6:51).

8. Jesus' last fourfold testament is all focused on love. The washing of the feet is the example of loving service. The command is a command to love. The Spirit who is given is a principle of union in the Church; in the second, third and fourth Eucharistic Prayers of the Roman Catholic rite, after the words of consecration, the priest prays that those who receive Jesus in holy communion may 'be brought together in unity by the Holy Spirit' (EP 2). The Holy Eucharist is the sacrament of unity: 'because there is one bread, we who are many are one body, for we all partake of the one bread' (1 Cor 10:17). The typical Christian virtue is love. The greatest infidelity in a Christian, the sin of which he should be most ashamed, is failure to love.

From the Spiritual Exercises of St Ignatius:

The preparatory prayer is as usual (n.190).

The first prelude consists of recalling the facts: how Christ our Lord, after sending two disciples from Bethany to Jerusalem to prepare for the Supper, followed later with the other disciples; how, after eating the paschal lamb and finishing the meal, he washed their feet and gave them his most holy Body and precious Blood; and how finally he spoke to them after Judas had departed to sell his Lord (n.191).

The second prelude is the composition of place. We should imagine the road from Bethany to Jerusalem—is it wide or narrow? level? etc. Then in the same way we should consider the supper-room—is it large or small? In one style or another? (n.192).

The third prelude consists of asking for what I desire. Here it is grief, compassion and shame that the Lord is going to his passion because of my sins (n.193).

The first point is to see those at the Supper and to try to gather some fruit for my own benefit from this consideration.

The second is to listen to what they are saying and in the same way to find something there for my own good.

The third is to attend to what they are doing, and to gather fruit from it (n.194).

The fourth point is to reflect on what Christ our Lord is suffering, or desires to suffer, in his humanity, according to the passage which is being considered. Thereupon I should begin to make a great effort and constrain myself to feel grief and sadness and to weep. I continue to exert myself in this way during the remaining points (n.195).

The fifth point is to consider how the divinity remains hidden; how it could destroy its enemies and does not do so, but allows the most sacred humanity to suffer so cruelly (n.196).

The sixth point is to consider that he suffers all this for my sins, etc., and what I ought to do and suffer for him (n.197).

I conclude with a colloquy to Christ our Lord, and at the end say the Our Father (n.198).

With regard to the colloquies, it should be noted, as we have already explained more briefly, that I should express a thought or a request which is in keeping with the subject-matter, that is to say according as I experience temptation or consolation, or desire one virtue or another, or seek to dispose myself in one direction or another, or as the subject of the contemplation prompts me to desire sorrow or joy. Finally I should ask for certain particular things which I most earnestly desire. In this way I can make either a single colloquy to Christ our Lord, or, if the subject or my devotion prompts me, three, namely to the Mother, the Son and the Father, as was indicated in Part Two in the contemplation on the Two Standards with the note which follows the Three Classes[1] (n.199).

Love

Love bade me welcome; yet my soul drew back,
      Guilty of dust and sin.
But quick-eyed Love, observing me grow slack
      From my first entrance in,
Drew nearer to me, sweetly questioning,
      If I lack anything.

1 See pp.106 and 111.

"A guest," I answered, "worthy to be here."
        Love said, "You shall be he."
"I, the unkind, ungrateful? Ah, my dear,
        I cannot look on Thee."
Love took my hand, and smiling, did reply,
        "Who made the eyes but I?"

"Truth, Lord, but I have marred them; let my shame
        Go where it doth deserve."
"And know you not," says Love, "who bore the blame?"
        "My dear, then I will serve."
"You must sit down," says Love, "and taste my meat."
        So I did sit and eat.

GEORGE HERBERT

19. THE AGONY IN
THE GARDEN

1. 'Could you not watch with me one hour?' Jesus asked his disciples in the Garden of Gethsemane (Mt 26:40). These words underlie the tradition of celebrating Holy Hour, when people pray for an hour before the Blessed Sacrament. In this meditation we pray simply for the grace to be with our Lord, for a while, in sympathy with his suffering, even though his suffering is now over.

2. Our Lord took with him into the garden Peter, James and John. They had been with him at his Transfiguration (Mt 17:1); he had taken them into the house with him when he restored the ruler's daughter to life (Lk 8:51). Now he wished them to be close to him as he wrestled with his desolation: 'Remain here, and watch with me' (Mt 26:38).

3. Jesus, who had always shown himself utterly fearless, now appeared overwhelmed with despondency and fear. He 'began to be greatly distressed and troubled' (Mk 14:33 RSV). There is much to commend the more violent version of the New English Bible: 'Horror and dismay came over him.' 'My soul is sorrowful', he said, echoing the question of Ps 43:5, 'Why are you cast down, O my soul?', adding the fateful words 'even to death' (Mk 14:34). Luke says he fell on his knees; Matthew says he fell on his face. Luke depicts Jesus' tension most graphically: 'Being in an agony he prayed more earnestly; and his sweat became like great drops of blood falling down upon the ground' (22:44).

4. Jesus' ambition in life has been to do his Father's will; he has

moved inexorably forward to this moment, having 'set his face to go to Jerusalem' (Lk 9:51; cf. 12:49–50). Now, in the most shocking form of the prayer given by Mark, he prays for release. 'Abba, Father, all things are possible to thee; remove this cup from me.' Still, he adds, 'Yet not what I will, but what thou wilt' (Mk 14:36).

5.   St Luke seems to indicate that this is one of the Temptations. St Matthew ends his account of the Temptations in the desert with the words: 'The devil left him, and behold, angels came and ministered to him' (Mt 4:11). St Luke at that point says nothing about the ministering angels, but concludes the statement that the devil departed with the ominous words 'until an opportune time' (Lk 4:13). The Agony in the garden seems to be the opportune time when the devil returns, and is vanquished again; for it is here that St Luke tells us that 'there appeared to him an angel from heaven, strengthening him' (22:43).

6.   The Epistle to the Hebrews seems also to carry an account of the Agony. 'In the days of his flesh, Jesus offered up prayers and supplications, *with loud cries and tears*, to him who was able to save him from death, and he was heard for his godly fear. Although he was a Son, he learned obedience through what he suffered' (Heb 5:7–8). The 'loud cries and tears' would be unknown to us, apart from this epistle.

7.   What caused Jesus so much anguish? Was it fear of the physical and mental suffering he could see coming? Was it a deep sense that his mission had failed or would fail? Was it a prophetic awareness of man's ingratitude? Was it a sense of carrying the weight of man's sins? Isaiah spoke prophetically in such a sense: 'The Lord has laid on him the iniquity of us all' (53:6). So did St Paul: 'For our sake he [the Father] made him [Christ] to be sin who knew no sin, so that in him we might become the righteousness of God' (2 Cor 5:21). Perhaps the

Agony of the fearless Christ is the clearest manifestation we have of the foulness of sin.

8.   St John tells of no agony in the garden; but his account of the events of Palm Sunday gives a glimpse of Jesus engaged in a mental struggle. 'Now is my soul troubled. And what shall I say? "Father save me from this hour?" No, for this purpose I have come to this hour. Father, glorify Thy name' (Jn 12:27–8).

9.   We might notice how Jesus' words at this climax of his life echo, or are echoed by, the words of the prayer he taught his disciples:

Jesus	*Lord's Prayer*
Abba, Father	Our Father, Who art in heaven
Glorify Thy name (Jn 12:28)	Hallowed be thy name
My Father assigned to me a kingdom (Lk 22:29) Remember me when you come into your kingdom (Lk 23:42)	Thy kingdom come
Not my will, but thine, be done (Lk 22:42)	Thy will be done
This is my body	Give us this day our daily bread
Father forgive them	Forgive us our trespasses, as we forgive . . .

E

Watch and pray that you may
not enter into temptation
(Mk 14:38)

Lead us not into temptation

Simon, Simon, behold, Satan
demanded to have you
(Lk 22:31)

Deliver us from evil

From *The Dream of Gerontius*

Praise to the holiest in the height,
    And in the depth be praise,
In all his words most wonderful,
    Most sure in all his ways.

Oh loving wisdom of our God!
    When all was sin and shame,
A second Adam to the fight
    And to the rescue came.

Oh wisest love! that flesh and blood,
    Which did in Adam fail,
Should strive afresh against the foe,
    Should strive and should prevail;

And that a higher gift than grace
    Should flesh and blood refine,
God's presence and his very self,
    And essence all-divine.

Oh generous love! that he who smote
    In man for man the foe,
The double agony in man
    For man should undergo;

And in the garden secretly,
    And on the cross on high,
Should teach his brethren, and inspire
    To suffer and to die.

Praise to the holiest in the height,
    And in the depth be praise,
In all his words most wonderful,
    Most sure in all his ways.

JOHN HENRY NEWMAN

20–22 GOOD FRIDAY

1. It is hardly necessary to summarize here the events of Christ's Passion and death. Each can read the New Testament accounts for himself and derive from them plenty of food for prayer. (In doing this it may be better to keep to one Gospel at a time, rather than to be continually comparing one Gospel with another.) What are given here are simply certain considerations which can form a background to prayer about the Passion. The amount of time which should be devoted to this prayer is the equivalent of three sections.

2. The grace that I ask is to know Jesus more clearly, love him more dearly and follow him more nearly in his Passion.

For many centuries Christians have practised this devout contemplation of the suffering of our Lord. The great Passions of Bach were written in this spirit; so was Isaac Watt's hymn:

> When I survey the wondrous Cross
> On which the Prince of glory died,[1]
> My richest gain I count but loss
> And pour contempt on all my pride.

The hymn *Stabat Mater* gives a still more violent expression of the way the Christian enters into the Lord's Passion:

> Holy Mother, pierce me through,
> In my heart each wound renew
> Of my Saviour crucified;
> Let me share with thee his pain,
> Who for all my sins was slain,
> Who for me in torments died.

1 In the original version of this hymn, printed on p.117, the second line reads: Where the young Prince of glory died.

3. We might have favourite paintings which express the Christian's leap back in time to sympathize with his Lord in his sufferings. There is a painting by Velasquez depicting a little girl gazing sadly at Jesus as he is collapsed at the foot of the pillar at which he was scourged. So too in Michelangelo's last, unfinished carving of the Pietá. Our Lady is not alone in bearing her Son's body, but in the background there is a cowled figure, said to represent the artist himself, who not only looks sadly and lovingly at his dead Saviour, but helps the mother to support the weight of her Son.

4. Of course we cannot really transcend time. When we pray, we are in contact, not with the suffering or the dead Christ, but with him risen and living. He cannot experience his Passion all over again; we cannot become contemporaries of it; his human consciousness at the time cannot have been aware individually of each devout follower who would commemorate his sufferings. We pray to Christ risen, while contemplating Christ suffering.

5. 'You know that you were ransomed from the futile ways inherited from your fathers, not with perishable things such as silver and gold, but with the precious blood of Christ, like that of a lamb without blemish or spot' (1 Pet 1:18–9). We should remind ourselves that, as truly as our mothers bore us, Jesus suffered these things, and suffered them for us, and for us sinners. 'God shows his love for us in that while we were yet sinners Christ died for us' (Rom 5:8).

6. Although Jesus in a manner of speaking carried our sins, we should not think of him as a substitute for us who receives from his Father the punishment which should rightly fall on us. This

would entail a wrong conception of God the Father's justice: he is not one who insists on punishment, any punishment, even the punishment of the innocent. The New Testament writers see God the Father as one who (like Abraham sacrificing Isaac) makes the sacrifice of giving his Son into a sinful world, rather than as an angry God who is appeased by punishing his innocent Son. 'God so loved the world that he gave his only Son, that whoever believes in him should not perish but have eternal life' (Jn 3:16; cf. Rom 5:8).

7. We may sometimes, in bad moments, feel like rebelling: we did not choose to be redeemed in this violent way; why should we have to take up our cross and follow Christ? The answer of faith must be that we cannot conceive how miserable life would have been if we had not been redeemed; if we could conceive it, we would never ask that question. Nevertheless we have the choice whether we wish to be with Christ, accepting his redemption, or against him. No intermediate position is possible: there can be no human goodness without the cross. 'You are not your own; you were bought with a price' (1 Cor 6:19–20).

8. The time for decision-making is past. We may now, if we wish, offer up to Jesus, who suffered for us, any decision we have taken, and pray for courage and generosity in keeping it.

9. In considering the stages of our Lord's Passion, we might like to consider how, despite intense suffering and great injustice, he never turns in on his own suffering or indulges in self-pity or recrimination, but is seeking to touch the hearts of the people whom he meets: Judas, Pilate, the Good Thief, St John and his Mother, St Peter. 'Father, forgive them . . .' When there is no chance of eliciting a response of faith, he stands in silence.

10. It seems that he saw every stage in his suffering as the fulfilment of his Father's will expressed in the Old Testament

prophecies. When he exclaimed 'I thirst' 'to fulfil the Scripture' (Jn 19:28), and received the vinegar, the last prophecy was fulfilled, and he could now say, 'It is finished' (Jn 19:30).

11.   We might meditate on Is 52:13–53:12 as a commentary on the Passion.

12.   As is suggested in the *Stabat Mater*, we might unite ourselves with the suffering Christ by sharing in the experiences of his Mother at the foot of the cross.

13.   Although our most natural reaction seems to be sorrow and compassion, the liturgy also strikes a note of wondering joy at the greatness of God's love for us:

Through the cross you brought joy to the world.
(Roman Catholic Good Friday Liturgy).

Hail true cross, of beauty rarest,
King of all the forest trees;
Leaf and flower and fruit thou barest
Medicine for a world's disease;
Fairest wood, and iron fairest–
Yet more fair, who hung on these.
(Good Friday Liturgy)

The same feeling is expressed in Crossman's hymn:

My song is love unknown,
My Saviour's love to me,
Love to the loveless shown,
That they might lovely be.
O who am I,

That for my sake
My Lord should take
Frail flesh and die?

The same feeling of grateful joy is expressed in the continuation
of the passage from Romans 5 quoted above: 'For if while we
were enemies we were reconciled to God by the death of his Son,
much more, now that we are reconciled, shall we be saved by his
life. Not only so, but we also rejoice in God through our Lord
Jesus Christ, through whom we have now received our reconciliation' (5:10–11).

The Sacrifice

O all ye who pass by, whose eyes and mind
To worldly things are sharp, but to me blind—
To Me, Who took eyes that I might you find:
        Was ever grief like Mine?

The princes of My people make a head
Against their Maker: they do wish me dead,
Who cannot wish, except I give them bread:
        Was ever grief like Mine?

Without Me, each one who doth now Me brave
Had to this day been an Egyptian slave;
They use that power against Me which I gave;
        Was ever grief like Mine?

Mine own Apostle, who the bag did bear,
Though he had all I had, did not forbear
To sell Me also, and to put me there:
        Was ever grief like Mine?

For thirty pence he did my death devise,
Who at three hundred did the ointment prize,
Not half so sweet as My sweet sacrifice:
                   Was ever grief like Mine?

Therefore My soul melts, and My heart's dear treasure
Drops blood (the only beads) My words to measure:
O let this cup pass, if it be Thy pleasure:
                   Was ever grief like Mine?

These drops being tempered with a sinner's tears,
A balsam are for both the hemispheres,
Curing all wounds but Mine, all but My fears:
                   Was ever grief like Mine?

Yet my disciples sleep; I cannot gain
One hour of watching; but their drowsy brain
Comforts not Me, and doth My doctrine stain:
                   Was ever grief like Mine?

"Arise! arise! they come!" Look how they run!
Alas, what haste they make to be undone!
How with their lanterns do they seek the Sun!
                   Was ever grief like Mine?

With clubs and staves they seek Me as a thief,
Who am the way of truth, the true relief,
Most true to those who are My greatest grief:
                   Was ever grief like Mine?

Judas, dost thou betray Me with a kiss?
Canst thou find hell about My lips? and miss
Of life just at the gates of life and bliss?
                   Was ever grief like Mine?

See, they lay hold on Me, not with the hands
Of faith, but fury; yet, at their commands,
I suffer binding, Who have loosed their bands:
                Was ever grief like Mine?

All My disciples fly! Fear puts a bar
Betwixt My friends and Me: they leave the star
That brought the wise men of the east from far:
                Was ever grief like Mine?

Then from one ruler to another, bound
They lead Me, urging that it was not sound
What I taught; comments would the text confound:
                Was ever grief like Mine?

The priests and rulers all false witness seek
'Gainst Him Who seeks not life, but is the meek
And ready Paschal Lamb of this great week:
                Was ever grief like Mine?

Then they accuse Me of great blasphemy,
That I did thrust into the Deity,
Who never thought that any robbery:
                Was ever grief like Mine?

Some said that I the Temple to the floor
In three days razed, and raisèd as before.
Why, He that built the world can do much more:
                Was ever grief like Mine?

Then they condemn Me all, with that same breath
Which I do give them daily, unto death;
Thus Adam my first breathing rendereth:
                Was ever grief like Mine?

They bind and lead Me unto Herod; he
Sends Me to Pilate: this makes them agree;
But yet their friendship is My enmity:
     Was ever grief like Mine?

Herod and all his bands do set Me light,
Who teach all hands to war, fingers to fight,
And only am the Lord of Hosts and might:
     Was ever grief like Mine?

Herod in judgment sits, while I do stand,
Examines Me with a censorious hand;
I him obey, Who all things else command:
     Was ever grief like Mine?

The Jews accuse Me with despitefulness,
And, vying malice with My gentleness,
Pick quarrels with their only happiness:
     Was ever grief like Mine?

I answer nothing, but with patience prove
If stony hearts will melt with gentle love:
But who does hawk at eagles with a dove?
     Was ever grief like Mine?

My silence rather doth augment their cry;
My dove doth back into My bosom fly,
Because the raging waters still are high:
     Was ever grief like Mine?

Hark how they cry aloud still, Crucify!
It is not fit He live a day! they cry,
Who cannot live less than eternally:
     Was ever grief like Mine?

Pilate, a stranger, holdeth off; but they,
Mine own dear people, cry, Away! away!
With noises confusèd frighting the day:
                Was ever grief like Mine?

Yet still they shout, and cry, and stop their ears,
Putting My life among their sins and fears,
And therefore wish My blood on them and theirs:
                Was ever grief like Mine?

See how spite cankers things!—these words, aright
Usèd, and wishèd, are the whole world's light;
But honey is their gall, brightness their night:
                Was ever grief like Mine?

They choose a murderer, and all agree
In him to do themselves a courtesy;
For it was their own cause who killèd Me:
                Was ever grief like Mine?

And a seditious murderer he was;
But I, the Prince of Peace,—peace that doth pass
All understanding, more than heaven doth glass:
                Was ever grief like Mine?

Why, Caesar is their only king, not I:
He clave the stony rock when they were dry,
But surely not their hearts, as I well try:
                Was ever grief like Mine?

Ah, how they scourge me! yet My tenderness
Doubles each lash: and yet their bitterness
Winds up My grief to a mysteriousness:
                Was ever grief like Mine?

They buffet Me, and box Me as they list,
Who grasp the earth and heaven with My fist,
And never yet whom I would punish missed:
                Was ever grief like Mine?

Behold, they spit on Me in scornful wise,
Who by My spittle gave the blind man eyes:
Leaving his blindness to Mine enemies:
                Was ever grief like Mine?

My face they cover, though it be divine:
As Moses' face was veilèd, so is Mine,
Lest on their double-dark souls either shine:
                Was ever grief like Mine?

Servants and abjects flout me; they are witty;
"Now prophesy who strikes Thee!" is their ditty;
So they in Me deny themselves all pity:
                Was ever grief like Mine?

And now I am delivered unto death;
Which each one calls for so with utmost breath,
That he before Me well-nigh suffereth:
                Was ever grief like Mine?

Weep not, dear friends, since I for both have wept,
When all My tears were blood, the while you slept;
Your tears for your own fortunes should be kept;
                Was ever grief like Mine?

The soldiers lead me to the common hall:
There they deride Me, they abuse me, all:
Yet for twelve heavenly legions I could call:
                Was ever grief like Mine?

Then with a scarlet robe they Me array,
Which shows my blood to be the only way,
And cordial left to rèpair man's decay:
                    Was ever grief like Mine?

Then on My head a crown of thorns I wear;
For these are all the grapes Sion doth bear,
Though I My vine planted and watered there:
                    Was ever grief like Mine?

So sits the earth's great curse in Adam's fall
Upon My head; so I remove it all
From the earth unto My brows, and bear the thrall:
                    Was ever grief like Mine?

Then with the reed they gave to Me before
They strike My head, the rock from whence all store
Of heavenly blessings issue evermore:
                    Was ever grief like Mine?

They bow their knees to Me, and cry, "Hail, king!"
Whatever scoffs or scornfulness can bring,
I am the floor, the sink, where they it fling:
                    Was ever grief like Mine?

Yet since man's sceptres are as frail as reeds,
And thorny all their crowns, bloody their weeds,
I, Who am Truth, turn into truth their deeds:
                    Was ever grief like Mine?

The soldiers also spit upon that face
Which angels did desire to have the grace,
And prophets, once to see, but found no place:
                    Was ever grief like Mine?

Thus trimmèd forth they bring Me to the rout,
Who "Crucify Him!" cry with one strong shout.
'God holds His peace at man, and man cries out:
                    Was ever grief like Mine?

They lead Me in once more, and putting then
My own clothes on, they lead Me out again.
Whom devils fly, thus is He tossed of Men:
                    Was ever grief like Mine?

And now weary of sport, glad to engross
All spite in one, counting My life their loss,
They carry Me to My most bitter cross:
                    Was ever grief like Mine?

My cross I bear Myself, until I faint:
Then Simon bears it for Me by constraint—
The decreed burden of each mortal saint:
                    Was ever grief like Mine?

O all ye who pass by, behold and see:
Man stole the fruit, but I must climb the tree—
The Tree of Life to all but only Me:
                    Was ever grief like Mine?

Lo, here I hang, charged with a world of sin,
The greater world o' the two; for that came in
By words, but this by sorrow I must win:
                    Was ever grief like Mine?

Such sorrow, as if sinful man could feel,
Or feel his part, he would not cease to kneel
Till all were melted, though he were all steel:
                    Was ever grief like Mine?

But, O My God, My God! why leav'st Thou Me,
The Son, in whom Thou dost delight to be?
My God, My God—
                    Never was grief like Mine!

Shame tears My soul, My body many a wound;
Sharp nails pierce this, but sharper that confound—
Reproaches which are free, while I am bound:
                    Was ever grief like Mine?

"Now heal thyself, Physician; now come down."
Alas, I did so, when I left My crown
And Father's smile to feel for you His frown:
                    Was ever grief like Mine?

In healing not Myself there doth consist
All that salvation which ye now resist;
Your safety in My sickness doth subsist:
                    Was ever grief like Mine?

Betwixt two thieves I spend My utmost breath,
As he that for some robbery suffereth.
Alas, what have I stolen from you?—Death:
                    Was ever grief like Mine?

A King My title is, prefixed on high;
Yet by My subjects am condemned to die
A servile death in servile company:
                    Was ever grief like Mine?

They gave Me vinegar mingled with gall,
But more with malice; yet, when they did call,
With manna, angels' food, I fed them all:
                    Was ever grief like Mine?

They part My garments, and by lot dispose
My coat, the type of love, which once cured those
Who sought for help, never malicious foes:
              Was ever grief like Mine?

Nay, after death their spite shall further go;
For they will pierce My side, I full well know;
That as sin came, so Sacraments might flow:
              Was ever grief like Mine?

But now I die; now all is finishèd;
My woe, man's weal; and now I bow My head:
Only let others say, when I am dead—
              Never was grief like Mine!

GEORGE HERBERT

O King of the Friday
Whose limbs were stretched on the cross,
O Lord who did suffer
The bruises, the wounds, the loss,
We stretch ourselves
Beneath the shield of thy might,
Some fruit from the tree of thy passion
Fall on us this night!

From the Irish

O Deus, ego amo te

O God, I love thee, I love thee—
Not out of hope of heaven for me
Nor fearing not to love and be
   In the everlasting burning.

Thou, thou, my Jesus, after me
   Didst reach thine arms out dying,
For my sake sufferedst nails and lance,
Mocked and marrèd countenance,
   Sorrows passing number,
   Sweat and care and cumber,
Yea and death, and this for me,
   And thou couldst see me sinning:
Then I, why should not I love thee,
Jesu so much in love with me?
Not for heaven's sake; not to be
Out of hell by loving thee;
Not for any gains I see;
But just the way that thou didst me
I do love and I will love thee:
What must I love thee, Lord, for then?—
For being my king and God. Amen.

TRANS. GERARD MANLEY HOPKINS

PART FOUR: THE RESURRECTION

23. THE RISEN CHRIST

1. When Judas went out to betray Jesus, 'it was night' (Jn 13:30). When Jesus died on the cross, 'there was darkness over the whole land' (Mk 15:33). We recreate that darkness in the Easter Vigil; into it comes the light of Christ, symbolized by the paschal candle. So in this meditation we pray that we may know Christ more clearly, love him more dearly, and follow him more nearly in his triumph; that, just as we tried to be with him in his suffering, we may now be glad with him in his joy.

2. We might centre our prayer on Jesus' appearance on Easter Sunday to the disciples on the way to Emmaus (Lk 24:13–35). When they meet him, their despondency is changed to joy. 'Did not our hearts burn within us?' (24:32).

3. There is cause for joy in the thought that Jesus' suffering is now at an end. 'We know that Christ being raised from the dead will never die again; death no longer has dominion over him' (Rom 6:9). He still bears the wounds, which are identification marks because they reveal his love: 'See my hands and my feet, that it is I myself' (Lk 24:39; cf. Jn 20:27). But they are now not causes of sadness, but of rejoicing, reminders to prompt us to gratitude, like the scar of a soldier's totally healed wound. The Lamb that St John saw in his vision of heaven was 'standing, as though it had been slain' (Rev 5:6). So nails containing the grains of incense are set in the paschal candle as a reminder of the glorious wounds.

4. Jesus' acceptance of his Father's will has now been rewarded. He 'became obedient unto death . . . Therefore God has highly exalted him and bestowed on him the name which is above every name, that at the name of Jesus every knee should bow . . . and every tongue confess that Jesus Christ is Lord, to the glory of God the Father' (Phil 2:8–11).

5.   His 'exodus' is now complete (Lk 9:31), and he has now returned to his Father (cf. Jn 20:17).

6.   The Resurrection marks Jesus' vindication by his Father. He was 'designated [or 'constituted'] Son of God in power according to the Spirit of holiness by his resurrection from the dead' (Rom 1:4). When the Father raised Jesus from the dead, 'he has put all things under his feet and has made him the head over all things for the church' (Eph 1:22). It is only after the Resurrection that Jesus says: 'All authority in heaven and on earth has been given to me' (Mt 28:18).

7.   We saw in the meditation on the Paschal Shape of Life (p.113) that in St John's Gospel Jesus' glory already begins at Calvary. 'Glory' is the visible manifestation of God–in the desert it took the form of the pillar of light. Jesus' whole life is the self-revelation of God. But in St John's thinking God reveals his nature most perfectly in the glory of the cross. St Luke's Gospel views things differently. There it is the Resurrection which most fully expresses Christ's glory. Jesus asked the disciples at Emmaus, 'Was it not necessary that the Christ should suffer these things and enter into his glory?' (Lk 24:26).

8.   This phrase 'it was necessary,' 'it was fitting,' or an equivalent, is applied several times to the connection between the cross and the resurrection (e.g. Lk 24:44; Heb 2:10). Why was it necessary? That the scriptures might be fulfilled. Why did the scriptures have to be fulfilled? Because it was his Father's will expressed in the Old Testament. But why was it his Father's will? Was it an arbitrary decree? No, God does not behave arbitrarily. The cross must precede the resurrection because that is what the fulfilment of human potentiality demands. The nature God gave us contains the law that the grain of wheat must die in order to bear fruit. And why did God make man of such a nature? Perhaps because this above all is the image of God in man. Combining the viewpoints of Luke and John, we

can say that it is the nature of God to reveal his glory in self-giving love. To express this fact in human terms we need both the sacrifice of Good Friday and the fulfilment of Easter Sunday.

9. So we pray to share Christ's joy. We do not seek a self-centred light-heartedness, which is all too easy at this stage of a retreat, when the end is close, and the sombre mood of Part Three is over. We ask for an unselfish joy at the fact that Jesus is glorified. In the words of a French retreat-giver, 'Even more than meditation on the Passion, this part requires *great interior silence*. This joy is not the exuberance of a healthy temperament but the effect of the presence of the Spirit.' Such joy is a grace, which we must pray for. And even if we are tired and dry at this stage of the retreat, our prayer will be well made if it is a prayer for joy in Christ.

10. We might sum up our feelings in the *Regina Coeli:* 'O Queen of heaven, rejoice, for he whom you were counted worthy to bear has risen as he said? Pray for us to God. Rejoice and be glad, Virgin Mary, for the Lord is truly risen.'

From the Spiritual Exercises of St Ignatius:

THE RESURRECTION OF CHRIST: THE FIRST APPEARANCE

He appeared first to the Virgin Mary. Scripture does not actually say this, but implies it in saying that he appeared to so many others. For Scripture presupposes that we have understanding, as the text implies: 'Have you also no understanding?' [1] *(n.299).*

1 Mt 15:16. If retreatants are unhappy about the lack of an explicit scriptural basis for this incident, they could instead take the appearance to the women at the tomb as the subject for their prayer.

THE SECOND APPEARANCE (Mk 16:1–11)

1. Early in the morning Mary Magdalen, Mary the mother of James, and Salome went to the tomb, saying: 'Who will roll away the stone for us from the door of the tomb?'

2. They see the stone rolled away and the angel, who says: 'You seek Jesus of Nazareth. He has risen, he is not here'.

3. He appeared to Mary, who remained near the tomb after the other women left (n.300).

FIRST CONTEMPLATION: HOW CHRIST OUR LORD APPEARED TO OUR LADY

The usual preparatory prayer (n.218).

First prelude: the facts. After Christ died on the cross, his body remained separate from the soul, though still united with the godhead.[1] His blessed soul, also united with the godhead, descended to hell, from where, after rescuing the souls of the just, he returned to the tomb. Risen now, he appeared to his blessed mother in body and in soul (n.219).

Second prelude. For the composition of place one will take the construction of the tomb, and the place or the house of our Lady, considering the details etc., such as the room and the oratory (n.220).

The third prelude is to ask for what I desire. Here it is the grace

---

1 That Jesus' dead body remained united with his divinity was the opinion of St Thomas Aquinas (*Summa Theologiae*, iii.50.2). Not all theologians share this view.

to rejoice and be intensely glad at Christ our Lord's great glory and joy (n.221).

Easter

Rise, heart, thy Lord is risen. Sing His praise
    Without delays,
Who takes thee by the hand, that thou likewise
    With Him mayst rise;

That, as His death calcinèd thee to dust,
His life may make thee gold, and much more, just.

Awake, my lute, and struggle for thy part
    With all thy art.
The cross taught all wood to resound His name
    Who bore the same.
His stretchèd sinews taught all strings what key
Is best to celebrate this most high day.

Consort, both heart and lute, and twist a song
    Pleasant and long;
Or since all music is but three parts vied,
    And multiplied,
O let Thy blessèd Spirit bear a part,
And make up our defects with his sweet art.

The Song

I got me flowers to strew Thy way;
I got me boughs off many a tree;
But Thou wast up by break of day,
And brought'st Thy sweets along with Thee.

153

The sun arising in the East,
Though he give light, and the East perfume,
If they should offer to contest
With Thy arising, they presume.

Can there be any day but this,
Though many suns to shine endeavour?
We count three hundred, but we miss:
There is but one, and that one ever.

GEORGE HERBERT

24. OUR SHARE IN
THE RESURRECTION

1. The grace that we ask is that we may share in the joy of Christ because his Resurrection is ours: 'If Christ has not been raised, then your faith is futile' (1 Cor 15:17).

2. First we can think of the way in which, whenever Christ appears after the Resurrection, he brings to his disciples the sense of peace and joy: 'Peace be with you.' 'Do not be afraid.' 'Why do you doubt?' 'Why are you troubled?'

3. He gives us a share in his risen life. We can see this idea expressed in the Epistle to the Ephesians. To begin with, St Paul regards the Resurrection of Christ as the proof of the power of God to work in us: '. . . that you may know what is the hope to which he has called you, what are the riches of his glorious inheritance in the saints, and what is the immeasurable greatness of his power in us who believe, according to the working of his great might which he accomplished in Christ when he raised him from the dead . . . (1:18–20). In the following chapter however St Paul goes further; the Resurrection is not just the *proof* of God's good will and his power, which is *exemplified* in Christ's Resurrection, but rather the moment of Christ's Resurrection *is* the moment of ours. God works our resurrection by the same act by which he rolled away the stone and brought new life to Christ so that that body moved out from the winding clothes. 'God, who is rich in mercy, out of the great love with which he loved us even when we were dead through our trespasses, *made us alive together with Christ* . . . and *raised us up with him,* and *made us sit with him* in the heavenly places in Christ Jesus' (2:4–6). To express this idea St Paul invents a series of

new words beginning with the prefix *sun-*, meaning '*co-*' or 'with'. The idea is that Christ's Resurrection *is* ours: we are 'co-raised' with him.

4. The Holy Shroud of Turin appears to bear the marks of Jesus' wounded body, burned into the cloth. It seems unlikely that the Shroud is authentic, but it is at least an ikon of the energy of the Resurrection. That same energy is now ours.

5. Another way in which this is expressed in the New Testament is in the Epistle to the Hebrews. If we put together Hebrews 2:10, 5:9–10, 6:20, 10:19–20, 9:6ff, 4:14, 7:24–5, we have the picture of Christ who, like the Jewish high priest, enters through the curtain into the holy of holies bringing the blood of sacrifice for the forgiveness of sins. But Christ, unlike the Jewish high priest, only needs to do this once, and does it bringing his own blood. Christ's entry through the veil into the holy of holies prepares the way for ourselves. He is our Pathfinder or Forerunner, so that where he has entered, we can follow. He brings us with him. In other words, he is not just like a mountain guide going up himself first and *showing* others the way up, but the fact that he has gone up first *enables* others to follow too. One can think of the guide cutting footholes, putting in pegs for people's feet, securing ropes. Even that is short of the reality: we enter in *with* Christ.

6. St Paul has the same idea when he speaks of Christ as the 'first fruits' (1 Cor 15:23); or the 'first-born from the dead' (Col 1:18).

7. His glory is now ours (Jn 17:22–4). He is the second or last Adam (1 Cor 15:22, 45); that is, just as Adam was thought to have represented the whole race, and involved the whole race in his sin, so Christ involves the whole race in his Resurrection.

8.   We can think of the number of times our Lord requires faith in his Resurrection (Mt 28:17; Mk 16:14; Lk 24:25, 38, 41; Jn 20:24–9). Do we believe in Christ's Resurrection, not just as a fact, but as a source of hope and spiritual power for ourselves? This is the good news that we try to spread to others. Have we the faith to believe in it ourselves?

9.   We now live in the time of the Resurrection. The Christ whom we meet is the risen Christ, not the suffering Christ. Christ in the Church, in the sacraments, in our neighbour, is always the risen Christ because he is now risen and cannot suffer again. Yet at the same time there remains the paradox that in our suffering neighbour we still meet Jesus in his suffering.

10.   We might like to focus our thoughts on the second Easter Sunday appearance which St Luke recounts: excitement gives way to fear, and fear in its turn is allayed by the sight of the sacred wounds and by Jesus' everyday action of eating a meal (24:33–43).

From *That Nature is a Heraclitean Fire and of The Comfort of The Resurrection*

O pity and indig ⎸ nation! Manshape, that shone
Sheer off, disseveral, a star, ⎸ death blots black out; nor mark
Is any of him at all so stark
But vastness blurs and time ⎸ beats level. Enough! the
Resurrection,
A heart's-clarion! Away grief's gasping, ⎸ joyless days, dejection.
Across my foundering deck shone
A beacon, an eternal beam. ⎸ Flesh fade, and mortal trash
Fall to the residuary worm; ⎸ world's wildfire, leave but ash:
In a flash, at a trumpet crash,

I am all at once what Christ is, [|] since he was what I am, and
This Jack, joke, poor potsherd, [|] patch, matchwood, immortal
    diamond,
              Is immortal diamond.

GERARD MANLEY HOPKINS

25. AFTERWARDS

1. The last chapter of St John's Gospel begins with St Peter's words to six of his fellow disciples: 'I am going fishing' (21:3). 'We will go with you,' they reply. The excitement of the Resurrection is over. They have been sent out by the Lord, as he was sent by his Father; they have received the Holy Spirit and the power to forgive sins (Jn 20:21–3). What comes next? A return to ordinary life: 'I am going fishing.' And there, in their ordinary occupation, they met Jesus on the shore (21:4).

2. The same is true of us. God's grace has been playing all round us during the retreat. The time has come for us to return to our fishing. There, in our daily lives, moment by moment, we shall meet the Lord. When the disciples saw Jesus standing at the edge of the lake, they 'did not know that it was Jesus' (21:4). The grace we ask for in this meditation is that we may recognize him when we meet him in our daily lives, and greet him with love.

3. Love is not in essence a feeling of joyous warmth at the thought of the beloved, though we are right to associate such feeling with the experience of 'being in love' or a 'honeymoon period'. Love goes deeper than feelings. Two people long married, whose lives have become so closely intertwined that existence apart is unthinkable, can be quite unsentimental, indeed even critical, in their relationship. They illustrate the fact that to love is not in essence to have particular feelings, but to give oneself to another. So when we pray for the grace to respond with love to God as he presents himself to us moment by moment in our lives, we are not asking for a warm aesthetic glow in contemplating the beauties of creation; we are asking to be able

to recognize God's loving will for us at every moment of our lives, and the grace to carry it out.

4. This attitude of searching for God at every moment of the day is summed up in St Ignatius's famous prayer, the *Sume et Suscipe:*

> Take, O Lord, and receive all my liberty, my memory, my understanding and all my will. You have given it to me; to you, O Lord, I restore it. All is yours: dispose of it wholly according to your will. Give me your love and your grace, for that is enough for me.

5. My love of God is my response to God who has loved me first. My love itself is his gift. It may be helpful to draw up a catalogue of God's acts of love. First, my life-history, my personal salvation-history, which mirrors microscopically the salvation-history of the Israelites. I should include in this spiritual autobiography the graces and lights God has given me in this retreat.

6. Secondly, I may think of God's creative and providential presence in every person and every thing with which I come in contact. 'In everything God works for good with those who love him . . . Who shall separate us from the love of Christ? Shall tribulation, or distress, or persecution, or famine, or nakedness, or peril, or sword? . . . For I am sure that neither death, nor life, nor angels, nor principalities, nor things present, nor things to come . . . will be able to separate us from the love of God in Christ Jesus our Lord' (Rom 8:28, 35, 38, 39).

7. If God's gifts are so wonderful, what must the giver be like? Created things are not only the work of the Creator, not only the self-expression of his imagination; they owe their being and their beauty to sharing in his own. 'Every good endowment and every

perfect gift is from above, coming down from the Father of lights' (James 1:17). If his creation is so beautiful what must the Creator be like?

8.   I may finally remind myself of any resolution I may have made, and imagine the circumstances in which it will have to be fulfilled at the individual moments of my life. In this way again I shall be responding to God in love. I may end by praying for grace, and repeating St Ignatius's prayer.

From the Spiritual Exercises of St Ignatius:

CONTEMPLATION FOR OBTAINING LOVE

One should begin by noting two things:

First, that love is expressed in actions rather than words (n.230).

Second, that love consists in a mutual exchange: that is, the lover gives and shares with the loved one what he possesses or what he can give; and vice versa. Thus, if one possesses knowledge, he gives it to the other who does not possess it; so too with honours and wealth. Thus there is an exchange of gifts.

We begin with the usual prayer (n.231).

The first prelude, the composition, which is here to see myself standing before our Lord God, the angels, and the saints who are interceding for me (n.232).

The second prelude consists of asking for what I desire. Here I ask for an inward knowledge of all the good I have received, so that I may be filled with gratitude and in all things love and serve his divine Majesty (n.233).

First point: to call to mind the gifts of creation and redemption and other particular gifts, pondering with great affection how much our Lord God has done for me, how much he has given me of what he possesses, and finally how the same Lord wishes to give me himself, as far as he can, according to his divine decrees. Then I will reflect on myself and consider with much reason and justice what I ought on my part to offer and give to his divine Majesty—namely all that I possess together with myself. In the spirit of one who makes an offering with great affection I shall say:

> *Take, O Lord, and receive all my liberty, my memory, my understanding and all my will. You have given it to me; to you, O Lord, I restore it. All is yours: dispose of it wholly according to your will. Give me your love and your grace, for that is enough for me (n.234).*

Second point: to see God as he exists in his creatures, in the elements giving existence, in the plants giving growth, in the animals giving sensation, in human beings giving intelligence, and so in me giving me existence, life, sensation and intelligence, and likewise making me a temple, since I am created in the likeness and image of his divine Majesty. Then I shall reflect upon myself in the same way as in the first point, or in any other way which seems better. I shall do the same in each of the remaining points (n.235).

Third point: to consider how God works and labours for me in every created thing on the face of the earth—that is, his disposition is like that of one who labours—in the heavens, the elements, plants, fruits, cattle, etc., giving them being, preserving them in existence, giving them growth, sensation, etc. Then I should reflect on myself (n.236).

Fourth point: to observe how all these blessings and gifts come down from above. Thus my limited powers come down from the supreme and infinite power above, and so too justice, goodness, kindness, mercy, etc., as rays come down from the sun, and streams from their source, etc. Then I conclude by reflecting on myself, as has been explained above.

Finally we should make a colloquy and conclude with the Our Father (n.237).

The Kingdom of God
'In no strange land'

O world invisible, we view thee,
O world intangible, we touch thee,
O world unknowable, we know thee,
Inapprehensible, we clutch thee!

Does the fish soar to find the ocean,
The eagle plunge to find the air—
That we ask of the stars in motion
If they have rumour of thee there?

Not where the wheeling systems darken,
And our benumbed conceiving soars!—
The drift of pinions, would we hearken,
Beats at our own clay-shuttered doors.

The angels keep their ancient places;—
Turn but a stone and start a wing!
'Tis ye, 'tis your estrangèd faces,
That miss the many-splendoured thing.

But (when so sad thou canst not sadder)
Cry,—and upon thy so sore loss
Shall shine the traffic of Jacob's ladder
Pitched betwixt Heaven and Charing Cross.

Yea, in the night, my Soul, my daughter,
Cry—clinging Heaven by the hems;
And lo, Christ walking on the water
Not of Gennesareth, but Thames!

FRANCIS THOMPSON

Jesu Dulcis Memoria

Jesus to cast one thought upon
Makes gladness after He is gone;
But more than honey and honeycomb
Is to come near and take Him home.

Song never was so sweet in ear,
Word never was such news to hear,
Thought half so sweet there is not one
As Jesus God the Father's Son.

Jesu, their hope who go astray,
So kind to those who ask the way,
So good to those who look for Thee,
To those who find what must Thou be?

To speak of that no tongue will do
Nor letters suit to spell it true;
But they can guess who have tasted of
What Jesus is and what is love.

Jesu, a springing well Thou art,
Daylight to head and treat to heart,
And matched with Thee there's nothing glad
That men have wished for or have had.

Wish us good morning when we wake
And light us, Lord, with Thy day-break.
Beat from our brains the thicky night
And fill the world up with delight.

Be our delight, O Jesu, now
As by and by our prize art Thou,
And grant our glorying may be
World without end alone in Thee.

TRANS. GERARD MANLEY HOPKINS

EPILOGUE

Whether we have been making this retreat full-time for about eight days or part-time over several weeks, much will have happened. It is unthinkable that God will not have been responding with great generosity to those who have given so much time to the search for him and his will. Indeed, the fact that we have been searching is itself God's gift. 'You did not choose me, but I chose you' (Jn 15:16).

So despite our weakness, timidity and lack of generosity, we can be sure that during these days and weeks God's grace and his light have been playing round us. It is important therefore not to lose what we have been given; 'no one who puts his hand to the plough and looks back is fit for the kingdom of God' (Lk 9:62). Consequently it will be very useful before the retreat ends to write in a few lines a brief account of the new understanding which God has given us, together with a short statement of whatever decisions we took during Part Two. It is equally important to keep this summary somewhere where we shall not lose it, and to turn to it regularly to refresh our memories. It is all too easy to forget.

There is a well known practice of maintaining regular 'days of recollection', in which we turn again to the good news which the Lord has given us during the retreat, and try to 'rekindle the gift of God that is within you' (2 Tim 1:6). Perhaps every two or three months we might fix a day in which we find extra time for prayer, and in the spirit of prayer reread this summary of our retreat.

What we have been given is a pearl of great price. These few lines, which we have written at a time of clarity and freedom of spirit, are our best means of keeping hold of the pearl.

APPENDIX

Concluding Prayers

It may be found useful to conclude each meditation with a prayer (cf. p.13). The following are suggested.

The Memorare

Remember, O most loving Virgin Mary, that it is a thing unheard of that anyone ever had recourse to thy protection, implored thy help, or sought thy intercession and was left forsaken. Filled therefore with confidence in thy goodness, I fly unto thee, O virgin of virgins, my Mother. To thee I come, before thee I stand, a sorrowful sinner. Despise not my words, O Mother of the Word, but graciously hear and grant my prayer. Amen.

ASCRIBED TO ST BERNARD

Some retreatants may find prayer addressed to the Blessed Virgin Mary unfamiliar and hard to justify. Accordingly when my notes, or St Ignatius' text, suggests that she should be invoked in a prayer or a colloquy, they may prefer to pray instead to the Holy Spirit. One such prayer is given below.

Come, Holy Spirit

Come, Holy Spirit, fill the hearts of thy faithful, and kindle in them the fire of thy love.

Send forth thy Spirit and they shall be created. And thou shalt renew the face of the earth [cf Ps 104.30].

O God, who hast taught the hearts of thy faithful by the light of the Holy Spirit, grant that by the gift of the same Spirit we may be always truly wise, and ever rejoice in his consolations, through Christ our Lord. Amen.

The Anima Christi

Soul of Christ, sanctify me.
Body of Christ, save me.
Blood of Christ, inebriate me.
Water from the side of Christ, wash me.
Passion of Christ, strengthen me.
O good Jesus, hear me.
Within thy wounds hide me.
Permit me not to be separated from thee.
From the wicked enemy defend me.
At the hour of my death call me.
And bid me come to thee,
That with thy saints I may praise thee
For ever and ever. Amen.

ANON., *14th century*